"I have had the privilege of personally knowing Jen Wilkin for several years. She is a woman intoxicated by the God of the Bible and has written *None Like Him* by staring at his majesty. The soul is healed not by gazing at its broken pieces, but by gazing at the beauty of its Creator and surrendering to the 'I can'ts, but he cans.' I pray you melt into the relief of belonging to the One who is unlike any other as you read this book."

> **Matt Chandler,** Lead Pastor, The Village Church, Dallas, Texas; President, Acts 29 Church Planting Network; author, *The Mingling of Souls*

"In an upside-down world that has humanized God and deified man, Jen Wilkin brings us the best news imaginable: our God is infinitely greater, more powerful, more majestic, and more wonderful than we can possibly fathom. Jen calls us to lift our eyes upward, to earnestly contemplate his attributes, and to humbly acknowledge our own limits. As we do, our hearts will be filled with wonder and awe that such a God should stoop to save and love us."

> **Nancy DeMoss Wolgemuth,** author; radio host, *Revive Our Hearts*

"My wife and I love Jen Wilkin. She represents a rising generation of evangelical women discontent with the status quo, yet fiercely committed to the Scriptures. Her teaching is provocative without approaching compromise, revolutionary without seeking novelty. This book is rock solid, and it portends an encouraging future for evangelicalism."

> **J. D. Greear,** Lead Pastor, The Summit Church, Durham, North Carolina; author, *Gaining By Losing*

"Far beyond a Sunday school lesson listing the attributes of God, *None Like Him* evokes a sense of both familiarity and wonder around the characteristics of the Almighty we worship. This book puts us in our place, beneath the God of all and over all."

> **Kate Shellnutt,** Associate Editor, *Christianity Today* magazine, Her.meneutics

"This book made me want Jen Wilkin as my best friend. But far more than that, it made me grateful that Jen Wilkin's God is my God. Books that are this theologically rich while also being this funny, this personal, and this penetrating are rare. So don't miss this one."

> **Nancy Guthrie,** Bible Teacher; author, Seeing Jesus in the Old Testament Bible study series

"Many of us attribute to God the characteristics of our fallen earthly fathers. In this study, Jen walks us through a better foundation for knowing and relating to our Father in heaven—Scripture itself. *None Like Him* is a helpful resource that reminds us that 'the knowledge of the Holy One is understanding.'"

> **Wendy Horger Alsup,** mother; author, *Practical Theology for Women* and *The Gospel-Centered Woman*

"What happens when women learn about the attributes of God? They rightfully praise him for who he is! Jen Wilkin has written a helpful book introducing the attributes that belong to God alone, while revealing our own tendencies to try to produce counterfeits in others or ourselves. A better understanding of who God is builds our faith and helps to guard against damaging theology. Jen presses the reader to see how God's incommunicable attributes affect our own spirituality."

Aimee Byrd, author, *Housewife Theologian* and *Theological Fitness*

"This wonderful book is big on truth and big on God, which means it is very good for my soul. Jen's exploration of God's attributes and her reminder of all the ways I'm not God and don't have to be God ministered to me as a wife, as a mother, and as a Christian. If true wisdom starts with the knowledge of God and the knowledge of ourselves, then here is a book full of wisdom."

Trisha DeYoung, happy wife to Kevin DeYoung, author of *Just Do Something* and *Crazy Busy!*; stay-at-home adventurous mother of six

"Many of us believe that greater peace and self-awareness come from exploring our own psyche or learning what makes us tick. But Jen Wilkin believes that greater self-knowledge comes from knowing and reverencing the One who is knowledge himself. In *None Like Him*, she invites us to learn how God's nature transcends our own and why the difference between us is good news. In fact, it's the very best news."

Hannah Anderson, author, *Made for More* and *Humble Roots*

"In my ministry to college students, I am rarely asked questions about morality or theology. They ask for wisdom. Young people yearn to know how the world works and how to work well within it. Jen sets us on the right path by inviting us all to the essential starting point: awestruck-wonder at our Maker. We must see how the eternal connects with the mundane if our lives are going to be filled with a sense of meaning. This is a resource that I would love to see in the hands of all of our students."

Ben Stuart, Executive Director, Breakaway Ministries

None Like Him

None Like Him

10 Ways God Is Different from Us
(and Why That's a Good Thing)

Jen Wilkin

CROSSWAY®

WHEATON, ILLINOIS

Published in association with the literary agency of Wolgemuth & Associates, Inc.

Cover design: Connie Gabbert

First printing 2016

Printed in the United States of America

Trade paperback ISBN: 978-1-4335-4983-0
ePub ISBN: 978-1-4335-4986-1
PDF ISBN: 978-1-4335-4984-7
Mobipocket ISBN: 978-1-4335-4985-4

Library of Congress Cataloging-in-Publication Data

Wilkin, Jen, 1969–
　　None like Him : 10 ways God is different from us (and why that's a good thing) / Jen Wilkin.
　　　pages cm
　　Includes bibliographical references and index.
　　ISBN 978-1-4335-4983-0 (tp)
　　1. God (Christianity)—Attributes. 2. Christian women—Religious life. I. Title.
BT130.W55　　　　2016
231'.4—dc23　　　　　　　　　　　　　　　　　　　　　　　　　2015032435

Crossway is a publishing ministry of Good News Publishers.

RRD　 27　 26　 25　 24　 23　 22　 21　 20
18　 17　 16　 15　 14　 13　 12　 11

Contents

On Becoming a God-Fearing Woman

Charm is deceitful, and beauty is vain,
but a woman who fears the LORD is to
be praised.

Proverbs 31:30

If you had told me five years ago that I would one day write a book for Christian women that led off with a quote from Proverbs 31, I probably would have punched you in the face. Arguably no chapter in Scripture is more over-referenced when it comes to addressing women, but stick with me as we teeter on the brink of cloying triteness. For the purpose of the business at hand, I think Proverbs 31:30 deserves a second look—for what it says about women, and more, for what it says about God.

In my mother's house hang two small, oval portraits of a man and a woman dating back to the late 1700s. They are David and Nancy Coy of Homer, New York, my great-grandmother's great-grandparents on my mother's side. We refer to them affectionately as "the ancestors," upstanding citizens of Congregationalist and Presbyterian stock, whose very frowns seem intent on keeping civilization from faltering. I take from their frozen expressions that life was not easy for them. Nancy, in particular, wears the look of a woman who doesn't get the joke. One suspects that if the artist had broadened his scope to include her torso, we would find her hands death-gripping a worn copy of the KJV. Like the portraits of other women of her time period, she is the very embodiment of the image we conjure when we hear the phrase "God-fearing woman." To call someone that today would sound archaic, maybe even tongue-in-cheek, but in Nancy's day it would have been recognized as high praise, a direct reference to Proverbs 31:30.

Today if we wanted to praise a woman as godly we would probably say something like, "She is so in love with Jesus," or, "She has such a deep walk with the Lord." The stereotypical portrait of this woman would be a soft-focus stock photo involving a field, filtered sunlight, out-flung arms, and a beatific smile, a little like a still shot of Julie Andrews from that opening scene in *The Sound of Music*. It's not a bad way to picture godliness, but it is quite a contrast to Nancy. And it leaves me wondering, in deference to Nancy, if there isn't some room for us modern women to ask what has happened to our idea of being a "God-fearing woman." I'm not suggesting Nancy knew a better version. I'm actually wondering if a more accurate conception of a God-fearing woman lives somewhere between a solemn scowl and a saccharine smile.

A somewhat less-than-shocking confession at this point: If I had to choose a verse from the Bible that has impacted me the most, it wouldn't be found in chapter 31 of Proverbs. It

would be Psalm 111:10. I came across it during my early twen-
ties, a time during which I sensed I desperately needed to grow
in wisdom but lacked a clear idea of where to start. Should I
study theology? Get a mentor? Memorize Scripture? My faith
at that time was primarily shaped by a feeling: my deep love
of God. But I knew I needed wisdom about how to follow the
God I said I loved. And one day in my reading, there was Psalm
111:10 answering my question of where to begin in a most unexpected way:

> The fear of the LORD is the beginning of wisdom.

I had to read it several times to let it sink in. The wisdom I
longed for started *where*? Of all the possible origin points for
wisdom, *fear* of the Lord was not one I would have come up
with on my own. This was not a verse that made me want to
cue the music, fling out my arms, and twirl in a field. The God
of my church upbringing was a snuggly Daddy-God, one who
I pictured to be much like my gentle and deeply affectionate
earthly father. The concept of fearing God was foreign to me.
How could the path to wisdom have as its starting point the fear
of the Lord? Scanning the verse, my eyes kept trying to replace
the word *fear* with *love*. Shouldn't the *love* of the Lord be the
beginning of wisdom? How could the Bible say in one breath
that perfect love casts out fear and then turn around and say that
fear was the first step toward wisdom?

My conception of God was that he was approachable and
accessible, the God that the Lord's Prayer endearingly refers to
as "Our Father." And he is that. He is mercifully and gloriously
that Father. But what the fear of the Lord acknowledges is that
he is not *only* that. He is also "in heaven," with a name that is
hallowed above all others. He is both a God who is near to us

and a God who transcends. The fear of the Lord comprehends the fact that the Father we are taught to call "ours" is also the Lord of the universe, enthroned between the cherubim, doing as he pleases among the nations.

Not all of us grew up with a snuggly earthly dad, much less a concept of an approachable Daddy-God. Despite knowing the grace of salvation, many of us still suspect that God (like Nancy) is perpetually scowling reproachfully in our direction. But the Bible paints for us a picture of a God who neither scowls nor coddles, a God who is both "Our Father" and "in heaven" in perfect balance. Finding that balance requires gaining a good working definition for how Psalm 111:10 uses the word *fear*. And for that, we can turn to the book of Hebrews.

The author of Hebrews takes care to distinguish between the fear of God's consuming wrath and the fear of God's holiness. Both may cause us to tremble, but only the second causes us to worship and repent. Because of Christ, you and I do not come cowering to fearsome, thundering Mount Sinai; instead we come expectantly to glorious, approachable Mount Zion (Heb. 12:18–24). We are exhorted to respond to this God by offering him "acceptable worship, with reverence and awe, for our God is a consuming fire" (vv. 28–29). Worshipful reverence and awe, not cowering dread, define a right fear of the Lord.

The worshipful reverence and awe of the Lord is the beginning of wisdom.

When we fear the Lord rightly, we do so not as those who are terrified of him. Christ, our Mediator, assures us that we may approach the throne of God with confidence. We do not tremble as the demons do; they rightly fear the wrath of God. Rather, we tremble as those who understand that God's wrath toward us is satisfied at the cross. When we fear God rightly, we recognize him for who he truly is: a God of no limits, and therefore, utterly unlike anyone or anything we know. This is the start of becoming wise.

But consider the inverted message of Psalm 111:10. Not only is the fear of the Lord the beginning of wisdom, *the fear of man is the beginning of folly*. This is the dual exhortation of Proverbs 31:30 that we need so desperately to understand:

> Charm is deceitful, and beauty is vain [the fear of man is
> the beginning of folly]
> but a woman who fears the LORD is to be praised [the
> fear of the Lord is the beginning of wisdom].

When we lose sight of the majesty of God, we invariably fill the gap in our vision with the fable of the majesty of someone else. We revere a spouse or a leader. We worship our children or a friend. We even give reverence and awe to ourselves. And this is complete folly. Not only is it unwise to give our worship to someone other than God, it is the very definition of irrationality. And it's an exhausting business.

So this is a book that hopes to reclaim the idea of the "God-fearing woman" from yellowed portraits in antique oval frames, as well as from the soft-filtered script-adorned frames of Instagram. In the pages that follow, I want us to consider the majesty of a limitless God. I want us to meditate on his perfections so that they become to us the most rational object of our reverence and awe. And along the way, I want us to stare down our tendency to ask others and even ourselves to be what only God is.

Life is too short and too precious to spend fearing the wrong things in the wrong ways. I propose we learn holy fear for a God like no other. Only then will our fear of man be put to flight, our self-adulation be laid to rest, and our hearts be turned toward worship. I want us to become *God-fearing* women in the truest sense of the word, to take our stand in gladness at the foot of Mount Zion, offering true worship to our Father in heaven. And in so doing, we'll make a beginning at becoming wise.

1

Infinite

The God of No Limits

Lord, we adore thy vast designs,
Th' obscure abyss of Providence,
Too deep to sound with mortal lines,
Too dark to view with feeble sense.

Isaac Watts

On the day I was born, the doctor who delivered me inscribed my birth records with a firm hand: seven pounds, eleven ounces, twenty-one inches. It was the first legally attested evidence that I was not God.

I would contribute ample proof to that effect in the ensuing years, but during the earliest moments of my life on February 4, 1969, well before I formed my first rebellious thought, uttered my first defiant syllable, or took my first disobedient step, the chasm between who God is and who I am had already been firmly established by the simple fact that I was measurable.

Any discussion of how God is not like us must begin with an acknowledgment that we are measurable and he is not. God is infinite, unbound by limits. He defies measurement of any kind. His limitlessness underlies all of his attributes; his power, knowledge, love, and mercy are not merely great, but they are infinitely so, measurelessly so. No one can place any aspect of who God is on a scale or against a yardstick.

This makes the task of writing a book about his attributes particularly daunting. One of my favorite hymns speaks to the measurelessness of just one of God's attributes: his love. The hymnwriter reflects on the futility of trying to capture it:

> Could we with ink the ocean fill,
>   And were the skies of parchment made;
> Were every stalk on earth a quill,
>   And every man a scribe by trade;
> To write the love of God above
>   Would drain the ocean dry;
> Nor could the scroll contain the whole,
>   Though stretched from sky to sky.[1]

I'm a feeble scribe working with scant ink and a very small scroll. And my task is to share at least a few meager insights about ten of God's attributes. Ten. I have never been more aware of my limits. But I want to do my part in this ongoing effort to describe the Indescribable. Faithful writers have done so for me. Stephen Charnock, Arthur Pink, A. W. Tozer, and R. C. Sproul have all explored the limitless character of God to my great benefit, and to lengths that I am not competent to go. But I hope in these pages to take the lofty view of God these writers have illuminated and ask a critical question:

"How should the knowledge that God is _____ change the way I live?" What measurable change should occur as a result of meditating on God's immeasurable attributes, as described in the Bible?

Why We Love to Measure

We limited humans are lovers of measurement; we number and count, quantify and track. If you were to look in your pantry, every carton would display the weight of its contents. Every food label would tell you the number of calories, fat grams, and carbs for a particular item. Your gas gauge tells you how much gas is in your tank. Your clock tells you how much time you have until dinner. Your budget tells you how much you can spend. Your social media account measures your circle of friends. We are happily surrounded on all sides by systems of measurement.

Our compulsion to measure is not a recent development. Ancient peoples tracked the movements of the heavens; their tools of measurement are still visible in canyon carvings and monolith rings. They measured tides and seasons, the passing of time. Measurement is the millennia-old obsession of the limited human, who, perceiving his own limits, seeks to transcend them by quantifying his world. That-which-we-can-measure we think we can to some degree control.

One of my favorite movies is *Hoosiers* (1986). It tells the story of a small-town basketball team from Hickory, Indiana, that finds greatness under the leadership of their coach, Norman Dale. The end of the movie is not hard to predict, and the '80s synthesizer music in the score is a trial for the nerves. There's also a scene in which Gene Hackman and Barbara Hershey earn the undisputable title of "Most Awkward On-Screen Kiss in the

History of Filmmaking." But at the 1:34 mark, the movie hits a note of brilliance.

Having reached the 1951 state finals, Coach Dale's team of small-town farm boys gets their first look at where the championship game will be played: a giant gymnasium, easily ten times the size of the small-town high school gyms they have played in all season long. As the players' eyes widen at the scene, Dale pulls out a tape measure. He asks a boy to measure and report the distance from the backboard to the free throw line. Fifteen feet. He asks two players to measure the distance from the floor to the net. Ten feet.

Smiling slightly, Dale notes, "I think you'll find it's the exact same measurements as our gym back in Hickory."

The scene is brilliant because it illustrates a universal truth: being able to take the measure of something is reassuring. It imparts to us a level of comfort and a sense of control.

We humans attempt to measure not just our environments but also our fellow humans. When we make a new acquaintance, or consider the viability of a political candidate, or interview someone for a job, we assess their strengths and weaknesses. We "take the measure" of their character and abilities, so to speak. We attempt to quantify their attributes, to judge how worthy they are of our trust or support and to keep our expectations realistic.

We also take the measure of self and others for the sake of comparison. Questions like, "Am I smart?" or "Am I rich?" or "Am I moral?" are answered with, "Relative to whom?" We choose our human yardsticks with care, often assuring ourselves that we will measure favorably by surrounding ourselves with people whose own shortcomings make us stand tall by comparison. We tell ourselves that compared to X, we are indeed quite smart, rich, or moral. But unless our measure of comparison is smarter, richer, and more moral than we are, we will preserve the myth of our own ascendancy. We will believe ourselves to be without rival. And that's where a measureless God begins to upend our sense of personal awesomeness.

Our Immeasurable, Measuring God

To the human mind, preoccupied with quantifying creation and its inhabitants, seeking control by measurement and validation by comparison, the Godhead presents a conundrum. The God of the Bible is infinite—immeasurable, unquantifiable, uncontainable, unbound, utterly without limit. We cannot take the full measure of him no matter how hard we may try. We cannot confine him to a physical or mental boundary. We cannot control him, and we can never stack up favorably beside him. Job's companion Zophar expresses our dilemma:

> Can you find out the deep things of God?
> Can you find out the limit of the Almighty?
> It is higher than heaven—what can you do?
> Deeper than Sheol—what can you know?
> Its measure is longer than the earth
> and broader than the sea. (Job 11:7–9)

David praises the infinitude of God's greatness:

> Great is the LORD, and greatly to be praised,
> and his greatness is unsearchable. (Ps. 145:3)

Solomon, too, acknowledges the limitlessness of God:

> But will God indeed dwell on the earth? Behold, heaven and the highest heaven cannot contain you; how much less this house that I have built! (1 Kings 8:27)

Paradoxically, he who is immeasurable is himself the measure of all things. Note this beautiful contrast in Isaiah 40:

> Who has measured the waters in the hollow of his hand
>   and marked off the heavens with a span,
> enclosed the dust of the earth in a measure
>   and weighed the mountains in scales
>   and the hills in a balance?
> Who has measured the Spirit of the LORD,
>   or what man shows him his counsel? (Isa. 40:12–13)

Put succinctly, who has measured everything? God has. Who has measured God? No one.

In striking paradox, God immeasurable concerns himself with measurements for arks and tabernacles, temples and cities. God unbound sets boundaries for oceans. He catalogs hairs on heads. He numbers stars and grains of sand. Our limitless God specifies the length of our limbs and the circumference of our crania. He measures our very days in handbreadths, lovingly and with intent. And all that he measures is perfect in measurement. All that he binds is perfectly boundaried. Yet he himself is infinitely detailed—limitless, measureless, unbounded.

The God of No Limits

What Zophar spoke, what David and Solomon worshiped, what Isaiah comprehended is this: God has no rivals. Not only that, but he measures and decrees the boundaries by which his creation will abide. Our whole lives as Christ-followers are to be given over to the identification and celebration of the limits God has ordained for us. He lovingly teaches them to us through his Word, through trials, through discipline. He humbles us through these means to remind us that we are not him, nor is anyone or anything else we know.

There is none like our God. The God of the Bible is incomparable, infinitely above his creation. To say that anyone or anything is like him is to try to express the unlimited in limited terms. Any comparison will fall short. Just as the authors of Scripture searched for adequate human language to apply to heavenly visions, we find ourselves ill equipped to express God's perfections. But we must still endeavor to try. Like the Israelites with their sandals still damp from the sand of the Red Sea shoreline, we feel the weight of the question that hangs in midair:

> Who is like you, O LORD, among the gods?
>   Who is like you, majestic in holiness,
>   awesome in glorious deeds, doing wonders?
>   (Ex. 15:11)

The psalmist, too, marvels:

> Who is like the LORD our God,
>   who is seated on high,
> who looks far down
>   on the heavens and the earth? (Ps. 113:5–6)

The answer, of course, is no one. Creation, existing within the limits of time and space, cannot rival, much less fully articulate, the splendors of a limitless God. Yet from our earliest moments, rivalry has been our intent.

Becoming Like God

As soon as my first child could crawl, he began exploring the limits of his world. What was he allowed to touch? What was off-limits? Any parent can tell you that if you place a small child in an empty room with twenty objects, nineteen of which he is allowed to touch and one he is not, an interesting phenomenon will take place. At first he may play contentedly with what is allowed, but before long he will turn his eyes toward the forbidden item. Soon he will begin moving closer to it, perhaps extending a hand toward it but not actually touching it. A gently worded warning may cause him to shift his gaze to his parent and reconsider his course, but eventually, barring physical intervention by that parent, he will almost certainly lay hands on the one object out of twenty he knows is not meant for him.

I remember trying to conceal my laughter when this process played out before me. The moral tug-of-war within my child was on full display, and it was comical both for its artless honesty and its familiarity. We do not outgrow the desire to test limits. With age, we may learn enough self-control not to put our drool-covered fingers in electrical outlets or write our names on the wall in permanent marker, but we still carry in us the same compulsion to do that which we ought not to do, to reach for that which we ought not to touch. We are line-crossers, boundary-breakers, fence-jumpers, carrying inside us a warped belief that our heavenly parent wants to withhold from us something that is needful or pleasurable. Even as we enjoy his good gifts, we feel a hyperawareness of the boundaries he has set, and we question their validity. Though he gives us nineteen gifts and warns us away from one danger, we suspect that what is withheld is not dangerous but desirable.

We see this exact pattern in the opening pages of the Bible. Lovingly placed in an environment designed for their safety and delight, our parents Adam and Eve mistook being created in the image of God as license to become like God. It was not enough to bear his image within the limits of human existence. No, only becoming like him would do. The Creator was holding out on them. But a crafty voice suggested that limitlessness was within reach:

> But the serpent said to the woman, "You will not surely die. For God knows that when you eat of it your eyes will be opened, and you will be like God, knowing good and evil." (Gen. 3:4–5)

So the finite reached to pluck the infinite from a low-hanging bough, and human history began its corrosive pattern of God-rivalry, pitting and eroding every peak and crevice of creation with the relentless repetitions of that first grasping, the long-armed reach of the human aspiring to the divine.

Reflect or Rival?

So it has been ever since: human beings created to *bear the image of God* instead aspire to *become like God*. Designed to reflect his glory, we choose instead to rival it. We do so by reaching for those attributes that are true only of God, those suited only to a limitless being. Rather than worship and trust in the omniscience of God, we desire to be all-knowing ourselves. Rather than celebrate and revere his omnipotence, we seek ultimate power in our own spheres of influence. Rather than rest in the immutability of God, we point to our own calcified sin patterns and declare ourselves unchanging and unchangeable. Like our father Adam and our mother Eve, we long for that which is intended only for God, rejecting our God-given limits and craving the limitlessness we foolishly believe we are capable of wielding and entitled to possess. Even as the redeemed, we crave the forbidden fruit of rivalry.

Theologians make two lists when they describe who God is. One list contains traits that are true only of God. The other contains traits that are true of God but that can also become true of us. Here is an example of such a list:

Only God Is	God Is (and We Can Be)
Infinite	Holy
Incomprehensible	Loving
Self-Existent	Just
Self-Sufficient	Good
Eternal	Merciful
Immutable	Gracious
Omnipresent	Longsuffering
Omniscient	Wise
Omnipotent	Jealous (for his glory)
Sovereign	Faithful
	Righteous
	Truthful

Every trait on both lists is limitlessly true of God. Once the Holy Spirit dwells in us, the list on the right can become true of us. It is a list we grow into as we walk in obedience to the commands of God. When we talk about being "conformed to the image of Christ," this is the list we are describing. It shows us how to *reflect* who God is as Christ did.

The problem I want to examine in the pages of this book has to do with how we humans treat the list on the left. Though this list can be true only of God, we want it to be true of us. It reveals how we try to *rival* God. We want this list to be true of us more than we want the list on the right to be. To see the truth of this, ask yourself two questions:

1. How many people spend their day plotting how to achieve limitless *love* for others?
2. How many people spend their day plotting how to achieve limitless *power* over others?

Though we know that the list on the right is for our good and for God's glory, we gravitate toward the list on the left—a list that is not good for us, nor does pursuing it bring glory to God. It actually seeks to steal glory from him. It is a list that whispers, as the Serpent whispered to Eve, "You shall be like God." It is the natural inclination of the sinful heart to crave this list, but as those who have been given a new heart with new desires, we must learn to crave the list on the right. The list on the right represents the abundant life Jesus came to give to us.

So this book will concern itself with the list of attributes that are true only of God. We will examine how we give our time and our efforts to chasing it, seeking to cast off the limits of our birthright as finite humans. And we will learn to trust this list to an infinite God.

We must recover the truth that was obscured by the Serpent: rather than being like God in his unlimited divinity, we are to be like God in our limited humanity. We are capable of bearing his image as we were intended only when we embrace our limits. Image-bearing means becoming fully human, not becoming divine. It means reflecting as a limited being the perfections of a limitless God.

Our limits teach us the fear of the Lord. They are reminders that keep us from falsely believing that we can be like God. When I reach the limit of my strength, I worship the One whose strength never flags. When I reach the limit of my reason, I worship the One whose reason is beyond searching out.

So it makes sense that our self-worship would so often take

the form of convincing ourselves that we are (or ought to be) limitless. But we don't just want limitlessness for ourselves—we tend to want it for others as well.

Why Honeymoons Never Last

It happens sooner or later in every relationship: someone will let you down. We have a term for the earliest stages of a relationship: the "honeymoon phase"—that rosy time period when everything but disappointment seems possible. We love the honeymoon phase because it requires no effort. The other person in the relationship has shown himself completely worthy of our love and trust, and we can't believe we spent so much time tolerating lesser relationships when this kind of connection was possible. It is a pleasure to lavish the other person with our affection. It will always be thus.

But then something happens—an unreturned phone call, an opinion we were not aware of, an annoying habit we had not noticed, a character flaw that hid, a weakness of some kind. A limit. We learn that our hero or our lover or our best friend does not possess limitless lovability. They are weighed and found wanting. And disappointment follows. We are faced with a dilemma: Will we try to force them back onto the pedestal they occupied during the honeymoon phase, or will we allow them to be, as the saying goes, "only human"?

I'm guessing this relationship cycle is familiar to you. We all experience it. Some of us had a father we thought was a superhero until we reached early adulthood. Some of us have had a close friend we thought was completely trustworthy, until she wasn't. Some of us have had pastors or spouses or political leaders whom we believed could never disappoint us—only to learn that they, too, had limits. It is no coincidence that we commonly speak of this kind of letdown as the toppling of an idol. When we ask another human to be unlimitedly trustworthy in any area, we are asking someone who is "only human" to be God.

This is why the Great Commandment takes such care to instruct us how to love those who are "only human." It tells a limited human to love God and others as limitlessly as possible. But to love self, others, and God as limitlessly as possible, we must learn to die daily to our propensity to measure and compare our limits.

Or, perhaps more accurately, we will have to learn to measure as God measures, to count as God counts.

He counts our sorrows. They are not infinite. They are measurable: countable, contained, recorded:

> You have *kept count* of my tossings;
>   put my tears in your bottle.
> Are they not in your book? (Ps. 56:8)

He measures our sins, yet his immeasurable grace exceeds them. Mercifully, our sins are finite in number, the product of finite beings:

> But where sin increased, grace abounded all the more. (Rom. 5:20)

He does not count our sins against us, because of Christ:

> Blessed are those whose lawless deeds are forgiven,
>   and whose sins are covered;
> blessed is the man against whom the Lord *will not count
>   his sin.* (Rom. 4:7–8)

And because of Christ, God urges us to learn to count others as Christ counted us:

> Do nothing from selfish ambition or conceit, but in humility *count others more significant* than yourselves. (Phil. 2:3)

He calls us to reevaluate the measures of our human successes:

> But whatever gain I had, *I counted as loss* for the sake of Christ. Indeed, *I count everything as loss* because of the surpassing worth of knowing Christ Jesus my Lord. (Phil. 3:7–8)

And he changes the measure of our adversity from curse to blessing:

> *Count it all joy*, my brothers, when you meet trials of various kinds. (James 1:2)

Could it be that this process of growing in the fear of the Lord is a simple matter of relearning how to count? By learning to worship God in his immeasurability, by learning to take the measure of ourselves, our sin, our circumstances, and others accurately, we might at last come to say with David, "The boundary lines have fallen for me in pleasant places. Surely I have a delightful inheritance." It's in that frame of mind that rivalry ceases and reflection commences.

Our birth records announce that we are limited. Our limitations are by design. Whether we spend the remainder of our lives denying or embracing this basic truth makes all the difference in how we will love God and others. I pray that, in the pages to come, a limited portrayal of a limitless God would move us toward greater dependence on our infinitely dependable God.

Note: At the end of each chapter you will find verses, questions, and a prayer prompt to help you remember and apply what you have read. Consider keeping a journal in which you copy or paraphrase each of the verses for meditation, noting what each adds to your understanding of the attribute covered in the chapter. Then journal your answers to the questions, as well as a prayer of response.

Verses for Meditation

1 Kings 8:27   Psalm 119:96   Isaiah 40:12–13

Questions for Reflection

1. What is your emotional response to the knowledge that God cannot be measured?

2. How have you attempted to "take the measure" of God? What limits have you placed (or wanted to place) on his character or will?

3. What God-given limitation or boundary do you most want to rebel against? How is that boundary for your good? For God's glory?

4. What person in your life needs you to accept his or her limits? What person in your life needs to accept yours? How might you set loving boundaries in that relationship?

Pray

Write a prayer to the Lord asking him to show you ways you have tried to "take his measure." Ask him to show you how your own limitedness can bring glory to him. Ask God to show you ways you have thought of him as having limits on who he is or what he can do. Praise him for his limitlessness.

2

Incomprehensible

The God of Infinite Mystery

Great is the LORD, and greatly to be praised,
and his greatness is unsearchable.

Psalm 145:3

Anyone who grew up in a small town can identify with the tru-ism that "familiarity breeds contempt." My hometown, while not terribly small, fits the model—we are fairly stunned when any of us makes good. I call it Small Town Syndrome. When you know a boy's mama and daddy, the church he went to, and the house he grew up in, and when you attend school with him from kindergarten through twelfth grade, you feel able to quantify the limits of his potential with a fair level of accuracy. You know who will probably never amount to much, and when someone breaks out of your expectation, the shock is enough to fuel local gossip for years to come.

A friend of mine grew up in the same small town as a now-famous Hollywood actor. When I asked if there were any early indications of greatness, my friend said she recalled little about him other than that he was handsome and widely regarded by the local girls as a "terrible kisser." (Now every time I see him kiss a woman on the silver screen, the romance of the moment is ruined as I search for any signs of revulsion on the face of his "kissee.")

I suspect that all successful people have those in their past who regard their success with a vague sense of contempt, having "known them when." And we can all relate in some measure to the experience of being discredited or undervalued by the people closest to us. Consider another target of Small Town Syndrome:

> [Jesus] went away from there and came to his hometown, and his disciples followed him. And on the Sabbath he began to teach in the synagogue, and many who heard him were astonished, saying, "Where did this man get these things? What is the wisdom given to him? How are such mighty works done by his hands? Is not this the carpenter, the son of Mary and brother of James and Joses and Judas and Simon? And are not his sisters here with us?" And they took offense at him. And Jesus said to them, "A prophet is not without honor, except in his hometown and among his relatives and in his own household." (Mark 6:1–4)

The people of Nazareth thought they knew Jesus. And in their familiarity, they held his teaching in contempt. They could not allow that he was anything more than they knew him to be. They believed their knowledge of who he was to be complete and accurate, and therefore found him easy to dismiss. They saw him as only a man, one whose measure they could take.

Knowing in Part

In the previous chapter we considered that God cannot be measured. Because we intend to learn more about God in this book, we must address how his limitlessness affects his knowability. Knowing who God is matters to us. It changes not only the way we think about him, but the way we think about ourselves. The knowledge of God and the knowledge of self always go hand in hand. In fact, there is no true knowledge of self apart from the knowledge of God. We cannot understand our human limitedness rightly until we see it compared to the limitlessness of God. By learning truth about him, we learn truth about ourselves. But how much do we know of him? Because he is limitless, the knowledge of who he is stretches to infinity.

God is incomprehensible. This does not mean that he is unknowable, but that he is unable to be fully known. It is the joyful duty, the delightful task of his children to spend their lives, both this one and the next, discovering who he is. According to Jesus, knowing God is the fundamental aim of life: "And this is eternal life, that they know you the only true God, and Jesus Christ whom you have sent" (John 17:3). We take pleasure in working to grow in our knowledge of him.

The truth of who God is surrounds us. Romans 1 tells us that all people have some knowledge of God just by looking around at creation. The Grand Canyon paints the contours of his character in broad brush strokes; majesty, eternity, omnipotence all announce themselves to the naked eye. But the believer, indwelt with the Holy Spirit, receives even deeper knowledge of God, found within the pages of the Bible. The Scriptures sketch his character with a fine-tipped pen for those who have eyes to see, elaborating across sixty-six books the story of who he is, what he has done, and what he will yet do.

But even with these declarations, God cannot be fully known by humans. Christians have meditated on the nature and character of God for thousands of years. Volumes have been written about God, but their sum does not contain the fullness of his attributes. The human mind in its finiteness cannot fully comprehend or express an infinite God. Even the most intellectually gifted theologian will barely scratch the surface of understanding who God is. He is fully known only to himself.

Put another way, the only expert on God is God.

Sufficient Knowledge

But fear not: though God is not able to be fully known, he is able to be *sufficiently* known. What we can know about him from creation and the Bible is sufficient for our salvation and our sanctification. Not only that, but it is more than sufficient in quantity to keep us in regular contemplation and reflection until we see him face-to-face. Were we able to know him completely, we would dismiss him. Because he is not able to be fully known, familiarity can never breed contempt.

During this life, we will not reach the end of our contemplation of God. Though we know him in part, we love him deeply. What we cannot know about him would only serve to increase our love for him were he to reveal it to us. No doubt we will spend eternity enjoying an ever-increasing revelation of the things we do not yet know about God. Because he is infinitely good, the things that we do not know about God are only good things.

We cannot say the same thing of each other. If you were able to learn everything you don't know about me, you would learn both good and bad. We all have skeletons in our closets. In a sense, God has a closet filled with infinite secrets about himself, but it contains only priceless treasures, no skeletons. The secret attributes of God, should we come to learn them, would bring us nothing but pleasure and assurance. The infinite unknown of God holds no faith-shattering duplicity, just a multiplicity of perfections waiting to be discovered across eternity.

Here again we see the vast difference between God and his creatures. Because God is infinite, he is incomprehensible, unable to be fully known. Because humans are finite, we are able to be fully known. And the implications of our knowability should change the way we live.

Toppling the Myth of Human Incomprehensibility

The first time I took a personality test was in college. It was the Myers-Briggs, a well-researched measuring tool that groups respondents into sixteen personality types based on their answers to ninety-four questions. I couldn't wait to get the results, and if you've ever taken a personality test I'm guessing you felt the same way. We love those tests because they tell us about our favorite subject: ourselves.

The results of my test were clear, placing me in a category that probably would not have surprised anyone who knew me. How I felt about the results was less clear. On the one hand, I loved gaining insight into how my preferences and judgments shaped my responses to the world around me. On the other hand, I was a little deflated to learn how predictable I was. How could a set of unremarkable questions so easily sort me into the correct bin? And why were there so few bins? Come to think of it, why were there bins at all? My perception of my own uniqueness, my "specialness," felt a little dented. Not only that, but the test assessed not just my strengths but also my weaknesses. I felt exposed. If the test could diagnose my shortcomings that readily, it seemed likely that everyone I knew could as well.

The premise of the Meyers-Briggs, and of all other personality tests, is that behaviors and preferences can be generalized. They find order in what we perceive to be random combinations of preferences and judgments. And they challenge our treasured belief that we are complex creatures. I believe they also point out how unlike God we are in a way we find unsettling: We humans want to think we are incomprehensible—unable to be fully understood—but we're not.

We are knowable. Completely.

But not by a personality test or by another person. Other people can gain insight into our strengths and weaknesses, our virtues and vices, by means of observation or by a tool like the Meyers-Briggs, but they can't know us fully. One reason this is true is because we are masters at concealment, even from those we love and trust. We excel at showing our finer qualities while carefully tucking away our shortcomings. And because other people have a limited interest in plumbing the depths of our character, we can get away with it. "Man looks on the outward appearance," and is content to do so, being so typically intent on his own hidden issues that he has little time to concern himself with the hidden issues of his neighbor.

No, our neighbor cannot fully know us, but far more concerning is that we do not and cannot fully know ourselves. One of the most frightening truths the Bible implores us to acknowledge is that we do not know our own hearts. Reflecting on this, the psalmist asks, "Who can discern his [own] errors?" (Ps. 19:12). The prophet Jeremiah warns that our hearts are characterized above all else by an internal, pervasive treachery that thwarts self-knowledge:

The heart is deceitful above all things,
   and desperately sick;
   who can understand it? (Jer. 17:9)

We don't know our own hearts. I am keenly aware of this truth every time I hear a sermon on the subject of sin. As the preacher warms to his topic about sin *X*, I begin compiling a mental list of all the people I know who need to hear this message and repent. I cull through lists of those who have offended me with sin *X*, plotting about how I can off-handedly relate the wisdom of this sermon to them and give sight to the blind. But how rarely, how belatedly does it occur to me that the message was for me? So unaware am I of my own sinful tendencies that I come to the sermon to sit in judgment on others, rather than to submit myself to judgment. So ignorant am I of my own bondage to sin *X* that I completely miss the word of correction being graciously extended—*to me*.

Knowable and Known

I want to believe I am the special case, the exception to every rule, the possessor of an extenuating circumstance that others are not aware of. When correction is offered to me, I tell myself that it is offered in error. If people really knew me, they would know that they are wrong to find fault. And my deceitful heart is happy to perpetuate this lie all the days of my life. Thank God, he allows no such thing. He graciously holds up the mirror of his Word, and my heart is laid bare. I am reminded that I am fully knowable, fully known.

God is not only an expert on God. He is also an expert on me.

O LORD, you have searched me and known me!
You know when I sit down and when I rise up;

> you discern my thoughts from afar.
> You search out my path and my lying down
>   and are acquainted with all my ways.
> Even before a word is on my tongue,
>   behold, O Lord, you know it altogether.
> You hem me in, behind and before,
>   and lay your hand upon me.
> Such knowledge is too wonderful for me;
>   it is high; I cannot attain it. (Ps. 139:1–6)

He knows me fully—every thought and every intention, every perception and every judgment, every response to the world around me, no personality test required. He understands my biggest strengths and my besetting sins. Even the temptations I face are so known to him that he calls them "common to man" (1 Cor. 10:13). Apprehending with complete accuracy the best and the worst of me, he is neither impressed nor horrified. He accepts me as I am because of Christ. Nothing is hidden before the One who formed my inmost being, and because I am fully known, I am fully free to love the God I know only in part. Though I do not know him fully, what little I do know is cause for the deepest love the human heart can produce.

And out of this love, I learn to trade the myth of human incomprehensibility for the mercy of human knowability. I learn to trust the expertise of God.

Divine Expertise

No, I am not an expert on my neighbor. Only God is. It may feel good to be quick to diagnose my neighbor's faults and prescribe a course of treatment, but my desperately wicked heart deceives me with the lie that I have any skill to do so. Recognizing this should help me walk in compassion toward those around me.

Rather than assuming I understand their motives and their difficulties, I can assume that neither I nor they can fully diagnose the problem. But God can. And then I can be quick to intercede for them instead of to judge. If I am fully known and not rejected by God, how much more ought I to extend grace to my neighbor, whom I know only in part?

No, I am not an expert on myself. Only God is. His Word gives a true diagnosis of my state, expertly shepherding my thoughts and intentions toward the path of life. Recognizing this should help me remain keenly aware of my propensity to believe my own self-promoting version of who I am. I must remember that the sermon has a word of correction for me before I look to apply it to someone else.

And no, I am not an expert on God. Only God is. Such knowledge should cause me to worship. The depths of the riches and wisdom and knowledge of God should bring me to my knees. His unsearchable judgments and inscrutable ways should inspire right reverence. And the glorious fact that he makes himself known in ways my finite understanding can grasp should cause me to celebrate, to devote my life to the joyful duty of discovering what he has made known of himself.

He reveals himself to those who seek him, and in seeing who he is, we see ourselves more clearly.

One day we will see God more clearly than earthly reason now allows and more extensively than his works and words currently reveal him. Though now we know in part, one day we will know fully, even as we have been fully known (1 Cor. 13:12). We will still be finite creatures seeking to comprehend the infinite, but we will at last be able to see him without the murkiness of sin blurring our vision. We will have eternity to progressively explore his perfections. And because to know him is to love him, our ever-expanding vision will elicit ever-expanding love. Like a Christmas morning with always another present to unwrap, eternity will increasingly disclose his hidden glories to the eyes of our hearts. And until then, let us pursue with eagerness what we can know of him in this life. I pray the chapters that follow will help us do just that.

Verses for Meditation

Job 11:7–9   Psalm 147:5

Psalm 145:3   Romans 11:33–35

Questions for Reflection

1. How does the knowledge that God cannot be fully known make you feel? List some positive feelings and some negative feelings. Explain your answers.

2. List three statements that you know to be true about God. How did you learn them?

3. Think of a time you felt misunderstood by someone. Why is it difficult to see and acknowledge our own sin in a misunderstanding? How should the truth that God knows you fully affect the way you respond in that kind of situation?

4. Think of a difficult person in your life. How well do you truly know him or her? How might acknowledging your limited understanding change the way you interact with him or her?

Pray

Write a prayer to the Lord acknowledging your partial knowledge of who he is. Thank him for specific ways he has revealed himself to you. Ask him for the humility to see yourself as a poor expert on him, yourself, or others. Thank him that you are fully known, fully accepted in Christ. Praise him that he exceeds your comprehension.

3

Self-Existent

The God of Infinite Creativity

All things bright and beautiful,
All creatures great and small,
All things wise and wonderful:
The Lord God made them all.

Cecil F. Alexander

"Isn't she so creative?" gushes my fellow baby shower attendee.

I survey the room, silently thanking the heavens that Pinterest didn't exist during my days of shower-hosting. The event is a marvel, meticulously executed down to the smallest detail. An average house has been transformed into a fantasy of hand-lettered, fondant-draped, glitter-encrusted, burlap-and-calico-beribboned splendor. Even the straws in the vintage glasses scream party-planning awesomeness. Our host has crafted a gathering so visually stunning that the actual arrival of the baby seems at risk of being anticlimactic.

Yes, I have to acknowledge, this girl is creative. By all evidence, she is able to walk into a craft store and, instead of curling up in the fetal position, begin to assemble magical combinations of paint, paper, and pipe cleaners in ways that inspire and elevate the senses.

I hate her.

Okay, I don't hate her—I admire her, begrudgingly. And I recognize that while I may not be the most creative shower host, I have been given other areas of creativity in which I have opportunity to shine. We all have. We call them our "areas of giftedness," and they are always linked to human creativity. A gifted musician creates arrangements of notes that elevate our sense of hearing. A gifted poet creates arrangements of words that elevate our emotions. A gifted chef creates arrangements of flavors that elevate our sense of taste. A gifted artist creates arrangements of colors that elevate our sense of sight. Even those of us who would not call ourselves extraordinary in any of these areas recognize our ability to combine several average things into something above average. We take piles of data and turn them into pie charts. We take collections of metal and turn them into machines. We take eggs, butter, cheese, and onion and turn them into an omelet. We all create. We are not creation-optional beings.

But the extent of our creativity is limited by the simple truth that we are human. You could even argue that no one who has ever drawn breath is truly creative at all. Not Michelangelo, not Debussy, not I. M. Pei, not even my friend, the Baby Shower Ninja. We are all hacks, arrangers of Someone else's palette of colors, wavelengths, and building blocks. The most creative human you know is a rip-off artist, shamelessly (gleefully?) re-arranging and recombining existing materials into new forms. No one has ever truly created anything.

No one, that is, except God.

God, Self-Caused

Unlike other books, the Bible does not take its sweet time to hook the reader. It stuns us with its opening line: "In the beginning, God created the heavens and the earth" (Gen. 1:1).

God, who is himself uncreated, creates everything. Gathering no materials, pinning no swatches to mood boards, consulting no color wheels, God speaks, and the universe leaps into being. From nothing he creates something. Unlike humans who create by rearranging what exists, God creates simply by the power of his word, and where there was once nothing, something miraculously appears.

Unlike everything God has made, he himself has no origin. No one gave him life. He did not begin to be; he has simply always been. Before he created everything we know (and billions of things beyond our capacity to know), he *was*, existing in completeness. He is self-existent, depending on nothing or no one to imbue him with breath. Though "in him we live and move and have our being" (Acts 17:28), he requires nothing or no one to have life. He "has life in himself" (John 5:26). He who has no origin is the origin of life for all.

A. W. Tozer captures this idea beautifully:

Man is a created being, a derived and contingent self, who of himself possesses nothing but is dependent each moment for his existence upon the One who created him after His own likeness. The fact of God is necessary to the fact of man. Think God away and man has no ground of existence.[1]

Derived and contingent. Utterly dependent. That's us.

Without origin, the source of all life. Utterly independent. That's God.

We humans must confess, "I am because he is." Only God can say, "I AM WHO I AM."

God: Set Apart and Owner of All

If you were to make two lists, one containing everything that was uncreated and another containing everything that was created, it wouldn't take you long to write it. It would look like this:

Uncreated	Created
God	(Everything else)

God has created all things, both spiritual and material. The angels celebrate him as worthy to receive glory and honor and power because "you created *all things*, and by your will they existed and were created" (Rev. 4:11). He did not create to fill a need or to cure loneliness or boredom. He created because it is his very nature to create. He is not a creation-optional God.

The implications of God creating everything are worth our consideration. First, we must conclude that God's creation is distinct from God. Unlike other religions, Christianity does not teach that creation is all a part of God himself. He is our origin, but he is separate from us. We are not pieces of the Divine. If we were, then the worship of creation would in some way be appropriate. Nature-worship and self-worship would be acceptable. Yet the Bible clearly denounces these things as idolatry.

Second, because God made everything, God owns everything. If everything created owes its existence to God, then nothing created truly belongs to another created thing. God does not own the cattle on a thousand hills because he purchased them. He owns them because he made them. Ownership implies rights and responsibilities. Because God owns everything, he is responsible for its care and has the right to do with it what he wishes.

Because we have created nothing and own nothing, we have no rights before our Maker, nor is there any way we can obligate him to us.

We have, however, been given rights and responsibilities with regard to one another. Because we are created in God's image, we possess both the right to life and the responsibility to protect it. No other human has the right to take life from us, because God is the origin and giver of life. We are guardians of the lives of others and stewards of a creation we inhabit but do not own. This is the picture given to us in Genesis 1 and 2: the man and the woman, two creatures placed in the garden of God's creation, charged with stewarding it and nurturing life. But since the fall, rather than seeing our world and our fellow man as entrusted to us for our care, we see them instead as objects of worship.

This is the message of Romans 1. When we look around at the created world, we ought to be moved to worship the One who made it. His hand in creation is unambiguous, to the point that to gaze on any part of it and think lofty thoughts of anything other than him is sheer madness. Futile thinking. Dark depravity. Inexcusable idolatry. "For his invisible attributes, namely, his eternal power and divine nature, have been clearly perceived, ever since the creation of the world, in the things that have been made. So they are without excuse" (Rom. 1:20).

Worshiping the creation rather than the Creator does not cause us to protect life or steward creation. It causes us to devalue life and consume creation. This is because all worship of the creation is actually a veiled form of self-worship. Consider abortion, human trafficking, domestic violence, and child abuse as daily evidences of our disordered worship of people. Rather than treating people as image-bearers, we treat them as consumable and expendable, only holding value insofar as they feed our desires. Dig through our landfills and gaze on our shattered landscapes to discern our disordered worship of things. Rather than stewarding resources, we treat them as consumable, expendable, only holding value insofar as they satiate our cravings. When we attach our worship to something less than God, we end up consuming and casting off the person or thing we worship in his place. And in the consuming and casting off, we reveal that the true object of our worship is self. We make a shameless declaration of "I AM."

Toppling the Myth of Human Creativity

Not only do we worship the creation in place of the Uncreated One, we convince ourselves that we are like him in his ability to create something from nothing. We confuse stewardship with ownership, viewing ourselves as givers of life.

We take the gifts that God has given us to steward—gifts like leadership, administration, and mercy—and we use them to fuel our "creator complex," employing them to build our own kingdoms instead of his. We look at the little kingdom we have brought into being and assert ownership over it: "I made this from nothing! I gave this life!" We begin to believe ourselves to be its creator and rightful owner.

In Daniel 4 we find just such a story. By the hand of the Lord, Nebuchadnezzar rises to great power as King of Babylon. One day as he walks on his palace rooftop looking out over his kingdom, his creator complex is exposed: "Is not this great

Babylon, which I have built by my mighty power as a royal residence and for the glory of my majesty?" (Dan. 4:30). We might shorten this brief speech even further to its most basic point: "I AM WHO I AM."

To which God essentially responds, "Well, no, actually, you're not."

Certainly Nebuchadnezzar has stacked existing stones into palaces, rearranged a palette of existing colors into hanging gardens, reordered existing power structures into a massive monarchy, but he has done so by the will of the Creator. He has not created something from nothing. And the Creator intends for him to recognize this truth. So God removes him from power, retracts the gifts he had entrusted to him, and lays him low in the dust from whence he came for a period of time. In essence, the lesson to be learned is this: "Okay, Nebuchadnezzar, we've seen what you can do with something. Now let's see what you can do with nothing." The once-mighty ruler descends into madness of the wild-haired, vagrant, grass-eating, claw-nailed variety.

When the time of the king's humbling is complete, his sanity is restored:

> At the end of the days I, Nebuchadnezzar, lifted my eyes to heaven, and my reason returned to me, and I blessed the Most High, and praised and honored him who lives forever,
>
>> for his dominion is an everlasting dominion,
>>> and his kingdom endures from generation to generation;
>> all the inhabitants of the earth are accounted as nothing,
>>> and he does according to his will among the host of heaven

> and among the inhabitants of the earth;
> and none can stay his hand
> or say to him, "What have you done?"
> (Dan. 4:34–37)

For many years I thought this story was telling us that God punished Nebuchadnezzar's pride by turning him over to insanity. But I see now that by stripping away his power and authority, God merely revealed the insanity that already operated behind Nebuchadnezzar's creator complex. It is sheer wild-eyed grass-eating madness to ascribe to ourselves the role of creator. But we do it all the time.

We do it with our families. We gave our children life, didn't we? We've spent the best years of our lives and the better part of our money creating a home and a future for them. They owe us their obedience and their worship. They had better make much of us by being successful and well-adjusted. So we scream, purple-faced from the bleachers when our kid doesn't perform like LeBron.

We do it with our jobs. We built this career from scratch, didn't we? We've poured our energy and talents into it across years. Without us, this company would be in serious trouble. We deserve every penny and every ounce of praise we get. So we become the boss who gives orders like edicts, or we turn in our notice, always moving to the next job because we're underappreciated and undervalued.

We do it with ministry. We saw the need and rose to meet it, didn't we? We gave selflessly of our time and our gifts. No one else could have made the impact we have. All this would never have happened without our sacrifices and our vision. We may not get the recognition we deserve now, but our heavenly mansion is going to be huge. So we take the credit for lives that are changed, and we stop hearing loving critique because, clearly, we have this ministry thing nailed.

Whatever our sphere of influence, we convince ourselves that we deserve credit for creating that which we are called to steward. We give worship to ourselves instead of to the Creator who made us and all we know. In fact, we require credit be given to us to validate our efforts.

Insanity. Madness. Full-blown delusion. To which God poses the simple question, "What do you have that you did not receive?" (1 Cor. 4:7).

All worship is owed to God, not because he demands it (although he rightly does), but because he made us. He is our origin. And anything good that we build or accomplish or "create" originates not in us but in him.

The Matter of Origins

Origins matter to humans. The *Antiques Roadshow* has held the interest of its viewers for over thirty-five years with a simple formula of determining the origins of items people have not properly valued. The side table found at a yard sale for twenty dollars that is actually an antique worth five hundred thousand. The thrift shop painting that turns out to be a van Dyck worth $673,000. Who made the item often determines its worth. It's enough to send us scrambling to our attics in search of hidden treasure. What might we have close at hand whose value we have underestimated?

That's a question worth asking, and one for which there is a ready answer. We have only to look in the mirror. Our value, yours and mine, derives from our origin. We often read Psalm 139 to bolster our self-esteem. But when Psalm 139 reflects that humans are fearfully and wonderfully made, it does so to raise our eyes from our mirrors to our Creator. It's a passage about *who* made us before it is a passage about what he made. It is an appeal to origin-based value.

What freedom is found in recognizing that only God creates! No longer must we labor under the delusion of our own self-importance. We need not find our value in people or possessions—it rests in our origin. We need not look to the success or failure of our pet projects as validation of our worth. We bear the mark of our Maker. It is not our job to be original, but to worship the Origin of All Things. We are free to explore the limits of human creativity to the glory of our Creator. We are free to love and cherish others at great expense without demanding their worship in return.

The Word Still Speaks Life

Furthermore, we are free to rely on God when our hope for a relationship or a situation has dwindled to nothing. Remember, our Creator-God specializes in bringing something from nothing. We cannot create hope where there is hopelessness or love where there is lovelessness. We cannot create repentance where there is unrepentance, but we can cry out to the God who can. In that first great act of creation, God miraculously rendered something from nothing. And he rejoices to continue that work in human hearts. God may restore a broken relationship or circumstance, or he may simply restore hope to you in their midst. Not everything will be made new in this lifetime, but his promise to grow in us the fruit of the Spirit means we can know abundant life whether relationships and circumstances heal or not.

The Gospel of John reveals the exact identity of the creative Word of Genesis 1:

In the beginning was the Word, and the Word was with God, and the Word was God. He was in the beginning with God. All things were made through him, and without him was not any thing made that was made. In him was life, and the life was the light of men. (John 1:1–4)

Jesus Christ, the one in whom life dwells, acted to create something from nothing in Genesis 1. And he is still doing so today: "Therefore, if anyone is in Christ, he is a new creation. The old has passed away; behold, the new has come" (2 Cor. 5:17).

God takes a heart in which righteousness does not exist, speaks the Word of life, and where once there was nothing, there is something: the righteousness of Christ. Where there was no righteousness, now there is his righteousness. We become new creations, created in Christ Jesus to do the good work of human creativity—applying the gifts he gives to reshape and reorder the sin-broken world he has charged us to steward.

Want evidence that God creates something from nothing? Look no further than your salvation. Each of the redeemed has known our Nebuchadnezzar moment, when our motives were laid bare and we were reduced to the right understanding that all we have has been given to us.

God graciously restores our sanity and raises us up to serve. Find great hope that the God of infinite creativity continues to do what only he can do. By all means, employ the gifts he has entrusted to you to create a home for your family, a career path, a ministry, but know that you do so as a steward. By all means, speak and act in a manner that points those around you toward the beauty of the gospel, but know that only God can create righteousness in the heart of another person. Find freedom in knowing that your human creativity is an echo intended to inspire worship of your Creator.

And then, create freely to your heart's delight.

Verses for Meditation

Genesis 1:1	John 5:26	Revelation 4:11
Exodus 3:14	2 Corinthians 5:17	
John 1:1–4	Colossians 1:15–17	

Questions for Reflection

1. Why is it important for us to understand that only God is uncreated?

2. What sphere of influence or authority are you most prone to take credit for having created? How has having a creator complex in these areas diminished your ability to steward your influence or authority?

3. Describe a time that God reminded you that without him, you are nothing and have nothing. How did that time change your perspective?

4. How does recognizing that God alone truly creates free you to embrace human creativity without sinful pride?

Pray

Write a prayer to the Lord confessing a "kingdom" you have believed you created with your own hands. Ask him to help you remember that your value lies in who created you, not in what you yourself create. Thank him that he is able to bring something from nothing.

4

Self-Sufficient

The God of Infinite Provision

Nor wanting, nor wasting, thou rulest in might.

Walter Chalmers Smith

I need thee every hour, most gracious Lord.

Annie S. Hawks

In 1989, the advertising world met a new icon in the form of a pink, furry, drum-playing bunny. Sporting blue flip-flops and shades, the Energizer Bunny marched across TV screens and billboards, accompanied by the tagline, "It just keeps going . . . and going . . . and going . . ." to indicate the seemingly endless supply of life we could expect from an Energizer battery. No need for a recharge or a replacement, that little pink rodent was a self-sustaining dynamo. So successful was the campaign that the term *Energizer Bunny* entered into our vernacular as a term to describe anyone or anything with apparently inherent limitless energy.

The Energizer Bunny tapped into a collective and long-standing human desire to design a machine powered by a perpetual energy source, one that never needs recharging or replacing. Though it no doubt had more ancient predecessors, the earliest recorded design for a perpetual motion machine dates to India in the 1100s. It was a wheel design, intended to stay in motion indefinitely once it was given a start. It was followed by numerous other designs, most of them wheels of some sort with counterweights, some designed to perform specific tasks (like move water) and some designed just for the purpose of exploring the idea of perpetual motion.

Even these earliest designs acknowledged the likelihood that the laws of physics would not allow for the possibility of such an invention, but even today we continue to be fascinated by the idea of a self-sustaining machine; as human "machines" that continually need the fuel of sleep, water, food, air, and rest—not to mention a host of other needs relational and spiritual—the thought that there might be a way to cast off at least some of these perpetual needs for perpetual needlessness is an enticing one, indeed. Take, for example, our current cultural obsession with caffeinated drinks as evidence of our desire to be sleep-optional creatures.

Without Needs, Yet Loving

Unlike the Energizer Bunny, we humans cannot "keep going . . . and going . . . and going." Only God can do that. Only God is self-sufficient. Our God is a God of no needs. What the Energizer Bunny purports to be, what the perpetual motion wheel aspires to be, God is in fact: a self-contained source of perpetual and perfect sustenance.

> The God who made the world and everything in it, being Lord of heaven and earth, does not live in temples made by man, nor is he served by human hands, *as though he needed anything*, since he himself gives to all mankind life and breath and everything. (Acts 17:24–25)

Creating and sustaining all things, he is himself created and sustained by none. For all eternity he is perfectly provided for in and of himself, needless of any aid, unflagging in strength, never hungry or thirsty, experiencing no lack. Nothing and no one outside of himself offers aid to him. Because he created everything, nothing he has created could possibly be needful to him for his existence. If it were, then like him, it would have always existed. Our God is self-sufficient, needed by all, needful of nothing.

Certainly not us.

This is news to some of us, who were taught to believe that God created humans out of a need for love or companionship. It sounds so good, doesn't it? The idea that his crowning act of creation was intended to fill a human-shaped hole in his transcendent heart. But there are no voids in his being, no gaps he must fill to be made whole. He is whole already, wholly loving and wholly loved within the perfect, eternal companionship of the Trinity. The Father has always loved the Son, who has always loved the Spirit, who has always loved the Father. No need for love or companionship prompted the Godhead to speak us into being. He created us gladly and he loves us infinitely, but he does not need us.

Nor do the Scriptures ever paint him as needing us. Imagine if God had greeted Abram in Ur with, "Abram, when I met you it was like my whole life came into focus. You complete me." Imagine if God had said to Moses from the burning bush, "Moses, you're such a gifted leader, wise and compassionate. I would be lost without you. You're my better half." These kinds of sentiments track well in romantic comedies and anniversary cards, but they are utterly out of place in our thinking about God. They are purely human in their expression. God has never and will never declare his need for us. It is for us to say, "I need thee every hour." It is for him to say, "I AM."

We need him every hour, but he needs us not at all. Certainly not for life, but also not for love or worship, not to bring him glory, not to bring reason to his existence. He is wholly provided for and wholly providing, and would be so had we never been formed of the dust.

This is actually the best news we could hear, because if God needed us in any way, we would most certainly let him down. Maybe not immediately, but eventually. Even the most consistent among us drops the ball more than we would like to admit. Praise God that his plans do not rely on my faithfulness, his joy doesn't hinge on my good behavior, his glory doesn't depend on my performance. I stumble along, chasing my own agendas and plotting my own ends, occasionally offering him the reverence he is perpetually due. He is unruffled and unharmed by my inconsistency. He is pleased to be glorified either through me or in spite of me, but he does not need me in the least. And yet he loves me, deeply and eternally, for no other reason than "according to the good pleasure of his will" (Eph. 1:3–6 KJV).

A Need Is a Limit

If God needed anything at all outside himself, he would be capable of being controlled by that need. A need is a limit, and as we have seen, God has no limits. Because he needs nothing outside himself, he cannot be controlled or coerced, manipulated or blackmailed by another who possesses what he lacks.

This is good news for us.

We humans know well the relationship between need and control. Think about hunger, for example. What happens when you get really hungry at a ballpark or theme park? Suddenly, you are willing to pay fifteen dollars for bad nachos and a soft drink. Why? Because the park manager knows that your level of need will influence your decision-making, and that you don't have other food options. The hungrier you are, the more you will pay the park's food vendors. Our needs influence our decisions. A need for money can influence us to steal. A need for intimacy can influence us to have an affair. A need for attention can influence us to talk in a certain tone or dress in a certain style. The greater our need, the greater our potential to be coerced or convinced into paying a steep price to meet it. Just ask an addict. Our needs weaken us in the face of temptation.

This is why when James 1:13 tells us that God cannot be tempted, we can believe what it says. There is no carrot to dangle before the Almighty. What can possibly tempt the One whose every need and desire is wholly met in himself? Praise God, no human possesses anything God needs, nothing with which to coerce him or manipulate him. I don't want you to have that kind of leverage with him, and I'm certain you don't want me to, either. We are kept safe from each others' divine blackmail by the self-sufficiency of God.

Why We Need

But we humans are remarkably needy, a reality we are eager to conquer or conceal. Americans, in particular, place a premium on independence. We love autonomy and view dependence as a sign of failure, a flaw of some kind, a lack of proper planning or ambition. Christians, in particular, can interpret physical, financial, or spiritual need as a sign that God has removed his blessing from us because of some failure on our part. But why do we take this view? It's almost as though our reasoning can't separate the presence of need from the presence of sin. But is sin the cause of human need?

A quick examination of Genesis 1–3 answers this question with a resounding no. In pre-fall Eden, Adam and Eve were created to need. Even before the fateful plucking of the forbidden fruit, they depended on God for the breath in their lungs, for the food in their bellies, for water, land, and light. They had needs, both physical and spiritual, before sin ever slithered into the picture. God created them needy, that in their need they might turn to the Source of all that is needful, acknowledge their need, and worship. Instead, they angled for autonomy.

Like them, we see human need as a flaw and human self-sufficiency as a crowning achievement. We become plate-spinners and ball-jugglers. With our lives collapsing around us, we paint on a smile and fake our way through another Sunday at church, denying our need for authenticity. We take out another line of credit, denying our need for financial stability. We ignore our symptoms of illness, denying our need for medical attention. We work late into the night, denying our need for rest. We starve ourselves to a size 2, denying our need for food. I'm fine. I'm better than fine. And I certainly don't need help.

We turn from the God-worship that should have resulted from seeing our need to the self-worship of believing we, like God, are self-sufficient. God, in his infinite wisdom, created us to need him. And he also created us to need each other. Genesis 2 reminds us that it was not good for the man to be alone. Rather, it was good for him to be in relationship. The New Testament expands this idea to include the fellowship of believers, comparing us to one body whose parts depend on each other, and for whom self-sufficiency is both illogical and unthinkable: "The eye cannot say to the hand, 'I have no need of you,' nor again the head to the feet, 'I have no need of you'" (1 Cor. 12:21).

We were created to need both God and others. We deny this to our peril. We are not needy because of sin; we are needy by divine design. Certainly, we can need in sinful ways, and we habitually confuse needs with wants, but we were not created to be self-sufficient. Nor were we re-created in Christ to be so.

Sanctification is the process of learning increasing dependence, not autonomy.

Unmasking Self-Sufficiency

What are the marks of self-sufficiency in the life of the believer? How can we know when we have stopped relying on God and others? When we deny our need for God, self-sufficiency reveals itself in the following ways:

- *Prayerlessness.* Our self-reliance causes us to cease approaching God with petition, praise, confession, or thanksgiving. Because we credit ourselves as the ultimate provider, we cease conversation with our true provider.
- *Forgetfulness.* Like Israel in the Old Testament, we forget the past undeniable provision of God. Like Israel, we trust our current and future needs to the idol of self, which we have adopted from the surrounding culture.
- *Anger in trial.* When difficulties force us to come face-to-face with our limits, we feel anger at our exposed need. We are unable to count our trials as joy (James 1:2),

seeing them as a verdict on our weakness instead of an opportunity to learn reliance on God.

- *Lack of conviction of personal sin.* We grow increasingly unable to acknowledge our personal need for forgiveness. When we hear a sermon or read a passage of Scripture, we hear it as a general admonition instead of a personal one.

When we deny our need for other believers, self-sufficiency reveals itself in the following ways:

- *Avoidance of Christian community.* Because we neither want nor believe we need help, we make no place in our lives for developing deep, authentic relationships with other believers.
- *Concealment.* When we must interact with other believers, we conceal the true state of our lives to preserve our autonomy.
- *Lack of accountability.* Believing our own lie that "we've got this," we grow increasingly unwilling to ask for or receive wisdom or correction from another believer. When we receive unsolicited feedback about our sin, we reject it.
- *Lack of humility.* Our growing self-reliance yields us increasingly unable to ask for or receive help from others, even when our need is obvious. When we receive unsolicited help, we feel embarrassment and even resentment.
- *Exhaustion.* Refusing to ask for or accept help, we overextend our limited physical and emotional resources, existing in a constant state of anxiety and weariness.

Toppling the Myth of Human Self-Sufficiency

It is not unreasonable to regard our vulnerability with unease. Our human needs are real, and we do not know in what manner or timing they will be met. The Gospels contain numerous stories of Jesus meeting physical needs in miraculous ways. He satisfied the physical hunger of the five thousand. He restored the sick to health and the lame to wholeness. He smoothed dangerous seas to safe waters. He even brought the dead back to life.

This same Jesus who, in his deity, miraculously met the needs of so many knew firsthand in his humanity what it meant to need. Human Jesus experienced the full range of human need. He needed food, water, air, shelter, clothing. He needed rest. He needed the community and comfort of his disciples. Even God in the flesh was not a human version of the Energizer Bunny. It is true that God cannot be tempted, yet Jesus, in his humanity, was tempted in every way as we are. And he set for us an example of how to respond to temptation borne out of need. Hungry and thirsty from forty days of fasting, weakened by his need, Jesus responded to Satan's offers of autonomy by affirming the all-sufficient will of his father. It's no wonder the Bible commands fasting from food. Fasting reminds us quickly of our need, of our utter lack of self-sufficiency. It's an express lane to relearning our limits.

And so is suffering, a truth to which Jesus also bears witness. In his greatest moment of physical need, in the excruciating suffering of the crucifixion, Jesus commended his spirit into the hands of his father. Why did Jesus feed and heal and resurrect and speak peace to the waves? Because in meeting those physical needs, he was pointing us to our far greater spiritual needs—in his greatest hour of physical need, he met our greatest spiritual need by dying in our place. By the punishment that was upon him, we are fed with the bread of life, healed from the sickness of sin, resurrected from spiritual death, and restored to peace with God. And we are joined to the community and comfort of the church.

Our greatest need has been dealt with once and for all. How much more will he supply all our lesser needs according to his riches in glory in Christ Jesus?

So set aside the plate-spinning, ball-juggling, pink bunny idolatry of self-sufficiency. Only God is self-sufficient. Only God has no needs. You have them, and so does your neighbor. Be quick to praise God for how unlike you he is in this. Be quick to confess to him your tendency to trust your own resources rather than acknowledge him as your provider. Be quick to confess your needs to him and ask him to meet them.

Not only that, but be quick to ask for help from others, and to receive it graciously when it is given. Be quick to offer to meet the needs of others before they have a chance to ask, including those outside the family of God. Who knows if by meeting some small need of theirs you might open a door to a conversation about their greatest need of all? The kingdom of heaven belongs to the poor in spirit. Its king meets us and saves us, not in our self-sufficiency, but in our lack. Blessed are those who need. And most blessed is he who supplies all our needs according to his riches in glory (Phil. 4:19).

Verses for Meditation
Psalm 50:7–12   Philippians 4:19
Acts 17:24–25   Hebrews 1:3a

Questions for Reflection
1. Why is it important for us to recognize that only God is self-sufficient?

2. What have you been tempted to believe that God needs from you? In what areas are you most prone to believe that you don't need him?

3. What human need do you resent the most? How is that boundary for your good? For God's glory?

4. Which of the marks of self-sufficiency discussed in the chapter have you seen in your own life? List them.

Pray

Write a prayer to the Lord asking him to show you how your own needs can teach you reliance on him. Praise him that he needs nothing, yet supplies every need. Thank him for meeting your greatest need through the work of Christ. Ask him to teach you to recognize the blessing of human need as a reminder of his ongoing faithfulness to sustain his children.

5

Eternal

The God of Infinite Days

From everlasting thou art God,
All time and space thou dost transcend!
The fullness of eternity,
Without beginning, without end!

Lowell Mason

You never know when a generation gap will blow up your dinner party. It was a rare family dinner—my husband, Jeff, and I, his parents, and his sister Emily and her husband were all gathered around my dining room table for the first time in a long time. Jeff's family is low on drama—everyone loves everyone else, and meals like these are always filled with laughter and talk. I had noticed that my sister-in-law was perhaps quieter than usual, but didn't think much of it. Then, in the middle of a lull in the conversation, her eyes locked on her water glass, she suddenly blurted out, "I got a tattoo."

A deafening silence. My in-laws, forks half-raised, gaping across the table. Jeff's eyebrows stretching for the ceiling. My brother-in-law studiously avoiding all eye contact. Me, feeling inappropriate hysterical laughter working its way up my ribcage.

"You got . . . a *tattoo*?" Jeff managed to repeat, no doubt remembering the two days in college he had an earring before learning he'd be paying his own tuition should it become a permanent addition.

More silence. Then my sister-in-law: "Well, you know I've always wanted one."

We did not. We did not know that. I could think of not one single conversation in which it had ever come up, and judging from the looks on my in-laws' faces, neither could they.

We still laugh ourselves to tears about that dinner. Jeff's parents, who are the most supportive family you could ever ask for, eventually made their peace with their daughter's decision. Emily had been wracked with anxiety to tell them, knowing they would be upset, so she chose what felt like the safest scenario to confess. And my in-laws, as much products of their own generation as their daughter was of hers, decided to get over it. I half expected Jeff to pierce his ear again now that the coast was clear.

We are all products of our generation, tightly bound to the history into which we were born. We inhabit a space of seventy to eighty years, and are shaped by the events they span. An age difference of thirty years can cause two people to see the same issue from completely different angles. We are creatures of a particular era, with limited perspective born of limited years.

In this, we could not be more different than God.

Unbound by Time

"'I am the Alpha and the Omega,' says the Lord God, 'who is and who was and who is to come, the Almighty'" (Rev. 1:8). The opening lines of the book of Revelation declare to us a God unlimited by time, so much so that he determines its beginning and its end. His eternal nature is written large and often across Scripture. The Bible begins with a time stamp, "in the beginning," and then spends sixty-six books describing the God who decrees seasons and times but is not bound by them in the least. Free to act within time as he wills, he exists outside of it. He is simultaneously the God of the past, present, and future, bending time to his perfect will, unfettered by its constraints. The past holds for him no missed opportunity. The present holds for him no anxiety. The future holds for him no uncertainty. He was, and is, and is to come.

Moreover, all of God's actions within time happen at just the right time. He is never early nor late, never subject to the tyranny of a deadline, never in a hurry, never playing catch-up with a schedule that has careened out of control. Ecclesiastes 3 tells us that he assigns "for everything . . . a season, and a time for every matter under heaven" (v. 1). But it doesn't feel that way from a human perspective. We look at the timing of events in our lives and think that perhaps, in at least a few instances, our timeless God has temporarily checked out.

We can readily acknowledge that there is an *appropriate* time for everything, but we have fairly formed opinions on when those times should be. The time to heal is any time someone is sick. The time to be silent is when I'm done speaking my mind. The time to die is at the end of a full life, not a moment before. But we see all around us that tragedy and comedy, birth and death, mourning and dancing present themselves seemingly at whatever time they choose. Human comprehension labors to make sense of it all.

Which is why the writer of Ecclesiastes goes on to say this: "He has made everything beautiful in its time. Also, he has put eternity into man's heart, yet so that he cannot find out what God has done from the beginning to the end" (Eccles. 3:11).

Put another way, God, who ultimately brings beauty from everything, has given time-bound humans a longing for timelessness, but in our limited understanding we cannot grasp what he is doing between time's beginning and its end.

We look around at the times and seasons and ask, "Where is the beauty God is bringing from this?" We expect him to make everything beautiful *in our time.* But the one who determines the beginning and the end does not operate according to our timelines. He will work all things according to his purposes. Every sorrow or harm we suffer will be redeemed for good. But sometimes it takes more than one lifetime for the ugly to be made beautiful. We may go to our graves without seeing the wicked receive their due. We may be laid to rest without finding forgiveness from a loved one. We may die without seeing the resolution of our own plotline, whispering with our final breath that we do not understand. No, we "cannot find out what God has done" even within the boundaries of our own birth and death, our own alpha and omega. But this does not mean that what God is doing is not perfectly timed. The problem lies not with his timing but with our perception of it.

Learning to Measure Time

Here I must acknowledge my great debt, not to a theologian but to a kindergarten teacher. Though she does not know it, Mrs. Greak, who taught four Wilkin children to write their names neatly and raise their hands politely, taught their mother a vital lesson about time.

She explained at meet-the-teacher night how difficult it was to teach the concept of time to a five-year-old. Each Monday she instructed the class to take out their journals and write at the top of the page: "Today is Monday. Yesterday was Sunday. Tomorrow is Tuesday." The class followed her instructions and harmony reigned.

Her difficulty began on Tuesday when the process was repeated. As soon as she gave the instruction to write "Today is Tuesday," looks of concern would flood her students' faces. With the instruction to write "Yesterday was Monday" a hand would go up.

"Mrs. Greak, you told us *today* is *Monday*."

"No, Monday was yesterday. Today is Tuesday."

More worried looks. Another raised hand.

"Mrs. Greak, you told us *tomorrow* is *Tuesday*."

"No, today is Tuesday. Tomorrow is Wednesday."

Following this pronouncement, the children would get upset. From their perspective Mrs. Greak had stated a complete contradiction: She had told them first that today was Monday and then that today was Tuesday. Which was it? Could this woman be trusted to teach them addition if she couldn't even nail down what day today was?

Of course, both statements were perfectly true. But because five-year-olds do not yet grasp the concept of yesterday, today, and tomorrow, they questioned her grasp on logic. The problem was not with the message. The problem was with the limited ability of the hearer to understand it.

We are like this.

We read the promise that God makes everything beautiful

in its time, and we look at the unresolved sorrows and hurts of our lives and the lives of others. And we begin to worry that the Bible cannot be trusted. We forget that we are receiving instruction from One whose perspective is not incrementally greater than ours, but infinitely greater. On a spiritual-insight scale from zero to God, we would be pathologically prideful to rate ourselves at kindergarten level. We must be neither surprised nor discouraged to find that we, who are of yesterday and know nothing, are at a loss to comprehend the timing of the One who transcends yesterday, today, and tomorrow.

We cannot expect to understand our own history or collective human history this side of glory, but we can trust our yesterday, today, and tomorrow to the One who was, and is, and is to come.

Living in the Present

Trusting God with our time means we make good use of the time we are given. This sounds simple, but it's not. Ephesians 5:15–16 tells us, "Look carefully then how you walk, not as unwise but as wise, making the best use of the time, because the days are evil." The King James translates "making the best use of the time" as "redeeming the time." We are commanded to be time redeemers, those who reclaim our time from useless pursuits and employ it to the glory of God. But how can we do this? I want to suggest three ways.

1. Let Go of the Past

Redeeming the time requires letting the past stay in the past. We can cling to the past by indulging in two different emotions: sinful nostalgia or regret. Sinful nostalgia causes us to idolize a time when life was "better" or "simpler," resulting in perpetual discontentment with our present circumstance. We may long for a time before bad news of some kind arrived, for a time when our health was better, when our kids were still young, or when a loved one was still alive. Life's changing seasons can cause a natural longing for the way things used to be, and though it is not necessarily sinful, it can become so. We are allowed to grieve the passing of happy seasons, but we are not allowed to resent their loss. There is a difference between missing the past and coveting the past. The antidote for covetousness is always gratitude: We can combat a sinful love of the past by counting the gifts we have been given in the present.

Regret, on the other hand, causes us to dwell in past mistakes or hurts, robbing us of joy in our present circumstance and often dragging us back into old sin patterns. As a child I learned to sing the words of Charles Wesley: "He breaks the power of cancelled sin, he sets the prisoner free."[1] How often have I needed those words as a reminder that the power of my past sins (or the past sins of others against me) is broken in Jesus's name. He replaces my historical liturgy of sin with one of holiness. When I become discouraged about giving in once again to a past sin, the "lifter of my head" reminds me that though I am not yet who I will be, I am not who I was. He draws me from the past back to the present with an assurance that sanctification is slowly doing its work *today*. He keeps me from rehearsing my past hurts by reminding me to forgive as I have been forgiven. We can combat the "bad news" of the past by remembering and trusting the good news of the gospel.

2. Let Go of the Future

Redeeming the time requires letting the future stay in the future. We can cling to the future by indulging in two different emotions: sinful anticipation or anxiety. We indulge sinful anticipation when we constantly covet the next stage of life. The teenager who wants to be a college student. The young mom who can't wait for her kids to be out of diapers. The woman in her fifties who can't wait to retire. Looking forward to the future is not wrong in itself. Seeing a future life stage as an escape from the present one is. As with sinful nostalgia, sinful anticipation is quelled by gratitude for the gifts we have been given in the present.

We feed anxiety when we live in dread of the future. We fear uncertainty or potentialities: the loss of a job, possible illness, or just the fact that we can have no idea of (or control over) what tomorrow holds. Our prayers become marked with requests to know the future rather than requests to live today as unto the Lord. Jesus reminds us not to be anxious for the future, "for tomorrow will be anxious for itself. Sufficient for the day is its own trouble" (Matt. 6:34). The antidote for anxiety is to remember and confess that we can trust the future to God. This does not mean that we make no preparation for the future, but that we prepare in ways that are wise rather than in ways that are fearful.

3. Live Today Fully

Redeeming the time requires being fully present in the present. We can squander today by feeding two different sins: laziness or busyness. Both the lazy person and the compulsively busy person subtly reject the God-ordained boundary of time. The lazy person believes *there will always be more time* to get around to her responsibilities. She can spend today as she pleases. She is characterized by procrastination, missed deadlines, and excuses. Like a profligate spender of money, she spends time without considering the cost, secretly believing she has an endless credit of hours. Laziness believes that the time God has given is not precious. We must redeem the present by considering the ant, as Proverbs 6:6 says, gathering when it is time to gather.

The compulsively busy person believes *there will never be enough time* to manage her responsibilities. She, too, believes she can spend today as she pleases, packing in more than one day's share of activity, complaining that there are not more hours in the day. She is characterized by exhaustion and over-commitment. Like a penny-pincher, she wrings every ounce of productivity out of every minute of the day, secretly believing that rest is for when we die. Busyness believes that the time God has given is not adequate. We must redeem the present by leaving time to observe the practice of stillness and the precept of Sabbath, taking on the trusting posture of one who sits at the feet of her Lord.

When we work to redeem the time, we reflect our Creator. God is the ultimate time-redeemer: He redeems all of time, and he redeems at just the right time. We are charged with redeeming the years he has given to us as a reasonable act of worship.

Toppling the Myth of Human Eternality

Tucked almost dead center in our Bibles is Psalm 90, Moses's splendid contrast of the eternal nature of God and the fleeting nature of man.

Lord, you have been our dwelling place
    in all generations.
Before the mountains were brought forth,
    or ever you had formed the earth and the world,
    from everlasting to everlasting you are God.
You return man to dust

> and say, "Return, O children of man!"
> For a thousand years in your sight
>   are but as yesterday when it is past,
>   or as a watch in the night. (Ps. 90:1–4)

Note the generationless, everlasting timelessness of God laid against the grass-and-flowers brevity of man. Unbound by time, God has always been and will always be. The years have no hold on him; yet he determines ours. Moses responds to this knowledge with a supplication: "So teach us to number our days that we may get a heart of wisdom" (Ps. 90:12).

Teach us. We have something to learn from your eternality and our ephemerality. Help us grasp the wisdom of numbering our days.

I was twenty-seven when I learned that my days were numbered. My insight came in the form of an unexpected phone call. Holding my six-month-old son, two months pregnant with my daughter, I listened uncomprehendingly as the doctor explained I had malignant melanoma, the deadliest form of skin cancer. They cut a section of skin, deep and wide, from the wall of my swelling abdomen.

Once you hear a cancer diagnosis, you can't unhear it. Even with successful treatment, it changes the way you number your days. I had been given an opportunity not many twenty-seven-year-olds could claim: the opportunity to count each of my days as precious. Any illusions I might have had that this life would last forever were effectively removed. I learned a perspective that many don't grasp until the aging process begins its faithful instruction in universal human frailty. I didn't have to wait for crow's feet or hip replacement. My eternal Father taught me young to pursue the sacred calling to "live this day well."

The experience marked me. Perhaps you can relate. Unlike my sister-in-law and the thousands of others of my generation who ink their credos into their flesh, I won't get a tattoo—not because I disapprove of them, but because I'm already sufficiently marked. I have a satin-slick scar which, if you were to see it, traces no apparent pattern. But to my eyes, more legible than any tattoo, it forms the words, "Tomorrow, if the Lord wills."

We live differently when we regard the future as a place we will go "if the Lord wills." God does not owe me the seventy or eighty years of which Moses speaks in Psalm 90. Every year he gives is a gift, gracious and undeserved. Thanks be to God, not just for the years he has preserved me but for the years he has ordained for me, perfect in number and known only to him.

How aware are you that your days are numbered? How willing are you to ask the Lord to teach you this precious truth? In the closing lines of Psalm 90, Moses makes one last remarkable request of God. He asks not once, but twice that our seventy or eighty years would have an impact that outlives their span.

> Let the favor of the Lord our God be upon us,
>   and establish the work of our hands upon us;
>   yes, establish the work of our hands!

Here is a remarkable truth: God is able to bring eternal results from our time-bound efforts. This is what Jesus intimates when he tells us to store up treasure in heaven rather than on earth. When we invest our time in what has eternal significance, we store up treasure in heaven. This side of heaven, the only investments with eternal significance are people. "Living this day well" means prioritizing relationships over material gain.

We cannot take our stuff with us when we die, but, Lord willing, we may feed the hungry and clothe the needy in such a way that an eternal result is rendered. We may speak words that, by the favor of the Lord, transform into the very words of life. This is the calling of the missionary, the magnate, and the mother of small children: spend your time to impact people for eternity.

Long after the beloved generations that debate tattoos around my table have gone to dust, long after your generation fades like grass, the God of all generations will endure. Thanks be to the God for whom "a thousand years are but as yesterday," the God who is from everlasting to everlasting. Thanks be to God for the limit of time, by which we are bound and he is not. Eternal God, establish the work of our hands.

Verses for Meditation

Psalm 90	Matthew 6:25–34	Revelation 1:8
Ecclesiastes 3:1–15	James 4:13–16	

Questions for Reflection

1. How have you been drawn to sinfully dwell in the past or the future instead of the present?

2. Which is the greater temptation for you: laziness or busyness?

3. If people are where we make eternal investments, which of your relationships most need your attention? List their names below.

Based on your answer, which specific uses of your time should you increase? Which should you decrease or eliminate altogether?

4. How aware are you that your days are numbered? How does your level of awareness affect the way you worship God? The way you love and serve others?

Pray

Write a prayer to the Lord confessing your desire to dwell somewhere other than the present. Ask him to help you number your days, treating each one as precious. Thank him for the good gifts he has given you today. Praise him that from everlasting to everlasting, he is God.

6

Immutable

The God of Infinite Sameness

Thou changest not, thy compassions they fail not
As thou hast been, thou forever wilt be.

Thomas Chisholm

My family spends vacation time at the home of my parents in
Santa Fe, New Mexico, a city nestled between mountain peaks.
Looming largest is Santa Fe Baldy, the tallest peak in view. Pueblo
Indians settled at its feet as early as 1050, but it is likely they were
not the first people to make the area their home. Often when I
wake up and look out at that mountain, I think about how that
exact view I am taking in has presented itself to the human eye
year after year, century after century. The jagged ridgeline whose
dips and rises I am learning by heart is the same one the earliest Native American settlers knew. The seasons may alter the
mountain face with foliage, snow, or shifting angles of sunlight,

but behind these cosmetic adjustments the great rock remains, its unchanging silhouette enduring across time. It anchors the landscape. It is the unchanging reference point upon which the eye fixes to determine the direction that leads to home.

The Scriptures speak of a God who does not change. Like the tallest mountain peak on the horizon, from generation to generation, God stands unchanging, immutable, anchoring the landscape of human existence as all else around him ebbs and flows, blossoms and withers, waxes and wanes. The Rock of our salvation endures. The sunshine and shadows of human circumstance may reveal certain contours of his character one day and different ones the next, but his character remains fixed. His plans remain steady. His promises remain firm. In an ever-changing world, he is the unchanging reference point upon which the inner eye fixes to determine the direction that leads to home.

"For who is God, but the LORD? And who is a rock, except our God?" (Ps. 18:31). The Psalms alone contain over twenty references to God as our rock, and the imagery permeates both the Old and the New Testaments. Jesus speaks of the wise man who builds on the rock instead of on shifting sand (Matt. 7:24–27). Through the prophet Malachi God declares, "For I the LORD do not change" (Mal. 3:6). The author of Hebrews exults, "Jesus Christ is the same yesterday and today and forever" (Heb. 13:8). James celebrates the goodness of the God "with whom there is no variation or shadow due to change" (James 1:17). He is immutable, not just unchanging, but incapable of change of any kind.

The Comfort of Changelessness

Consider how great the comfort in being personally connected to a God who changes not. From the Old Testament to the New, he is the same. None of his attributes can increase or decrease because each is unchangingly infinite. His knowledge cannot increase or decrease. His faithfulness cannot increase or decrease. Our actions, good or bad, can neither add to nor diminish his glory. He cannot become more holy or less steadfast. He simply is these things to the utmost—forever. The *God who was* is the *God who is*. The *God who is* is the *God who is to come*. The *God who is to come* is the *God who was*.

Because he does not change, we can rely on the unchanging truth of Scripture. What he pronounces as sin will always be sin. What he pronounces as good will always be good. All that he has promised to do must come to pass. The gospel itself is bound up in the idea of God's immutability. We fervently need God to stay the same—our great hope of salvation lies in his remaining exactly as who he says he is, doing exactly what he has said he will do. As long as his infinite sameness endures, he will not change his mind about setting his love on us. We cannot commit a future sin that will change his verdict, because his verdict was passed with every sin past, present, and future fixed in view. Whom God pronounces righteous will always be righteous. Nothing we could do can remove from us the seal of his promised redemption. Nothing can separate us from the unfailing, unchanging love of this great God, the Rock of our salvation upon which the house of our faith is built.

Changeable Creatures

Unlike our God of infinite sameness, you and I, his creatures, experience constant change in every sphere we inhabit. Our physical bodies grow and change, mature and decline. The dimples and rolls of babyhood become the wrinkles and cataracts of old age. Our physical beauty waxes and wanes. Our intellect expands and contracts. Our affections increase and diminish, as do our fears and aversions. Our circumstances change, and so do our allegiances. We shout "crucify him" while our cries of "hosanna" are even still ringing in the air. Our fashion sense, our taste in clothing, our political opinions, our financial status, our perceptions of others change year to year, and sometimes moment to moment.

Those grasping for the comfort of certainty are blithely reminded that the only certainty is change itself. Not a particularly comforting thought. But it's also not a very accurate one. It's closer to the truth to say that the only certainty is God himself, who changes not.

But because nothing you and I can perceive escapes change, grasping his infinite sameness can be a difficult task. We find it far easier to try to seek assurance in a tangible person or thing that at least gives a convincing impression that it is unchanging. Maybe we draw comfort from a friendship that has stood the test of time. Such a relationship may feel unchanging, but on closer observation we would note that it has matured and deepened. Maybe we draw comfort from a vacation spot that seems untouched by time every instance we visit it. But of course, if we looked closely, we would note the signs of change there as well.

My grandparents' house in Pittsburgh was a place where I always felt like time stood still. In that comforting dwelling, not a single knickknack ever stirred from its location. Every visit promised sameness—the same smell of creosote from the driveway, the same meals on the same dishes at the same table. After dinner, the same board games. The same evenings spent on the patio watching the fireflies. The same pink bathtub for soaking and the same antique sleigh bed for dreaming. Heaven.

On my last visit to Pittsburgh, I drove to their wooded cul-de-sac and parked at the curb. My grandparents had been gone for some time, but I wanted to see the house and remember. There was nothing to see but forest. A neighbor wanting a larger lot had purchased the house and had it torn down. It bothered me how much the change bothered me. How could someone bulldoze heaven, for heaven's sake?

Where Our Unchanging Hope Lies

The sadness or frustration we feel about changes to something that we believed to be unchanging reveals our tendency to ascribe what is true only of God to people, possessions, or circumstances that are not him—to expect earthy places to be heavenly. I tell myself that my love of routine and my aversion to change are a longing for the God who does not change, but if I am honest, they are just plain idolatry. In truth, I am telling temporary, changing things, "I need you to be God. Please just stay the same."

But the worst part is not that I ask the world around me not to change (or to at least act convincingly as though it is not). The worst part is that, when confronted with my own entrenched sin, my immediate defense is to say, "That's just who I am. I can't change."

I can't change. Immutable.

Lie. Lie from the pit of hell. Whether uttered in hopelessness or defiance, this statement is a lie. Only one person does not change, and that is God. But when faced with the need to turn from sin, I answer the question of "Who is unchanging?" with "I Am."

Just as my assurance of salvation rests in the fact that God cannot change, my hope of sanctification rests in the fact that I can.

What greater disavowal of the gospel of grace than to claim

it is capable of changing every sinner's heart but mine? What greater egotism? No doubt, as unbelievers we feel the hopelessness of our plight apart from grace. We rightly surmise that, without an intervening miracle, we cannot change for the better. But when the miracle of grace has been applied to our hearts, change becomes gloriously possible. The Unchanging One dispels forever the myth of human immutability, changing a heart that was once stone to a heart of flesh, changing desires that once sought only to glorify self to those that seek to glorify him.

Toppling the Myth of Human Immutability

Perhaps nowhere do we demonstrate more clearly our commitment to the myth of human immutability than in the way that we argue with each other.

"You never listen when I talk to you."
"You always leave your socks on the floor."
"You're never ready on time for school."
"We always have meatloaf for dinner."

That last one was leveled at me by a meatloaf-averse child. I assure you, we do not always have meatloaf for dinner. Do we frequently have meatloaf? Yes. Guilty as charged, small, ungrateful person in my home who does not have to plan the menu or prepare the dinner. Do we *always* have meatloaf? No. But that word *always* is so enticingly helpful when we want to bolster a weak argument. Why does someone always complain when I serve meatloaf?

When we apply the terms *always* or *never* to other people, we speak an untruth. Human beings don't *always* or *never* anything. We just aren't that consistent. We *frequently*, we *fairly regularly*, we *often* or *habitually*, but we do not *always* or *never*.

As finite and mutable creatures, we cannot lay claim to these terms, either as pejoratives or as praise. They can only truly be spoken of God.

This is why, when 1 Corinthians 13 is read at weddings (and it seems to be read at every wedding, whether the couple are proselytes or pagans), I have stopped wanting to giggle. I used to sit having a silent joke with myself as that gorgeous definition of love was read over the couple.

> Love is patient, love is kind. It does not envy, it does not boast, it is not proud. It does not dishonor others, it is not self-seeking, it is not easily angered, it keeps no record of wrongs. Love does not delight in evil but rejoices with the truth. (vv. 4–6 NIV)

Good luck with that, you two. It seems likely that the groom is going to habitually leave his towel on the bathroom floor. It seems possible that the bride is going to mention repeatedly that this is the case. How many marriages actually consistently demonstrate the kind of love described in 1 Corinthians 13? I mean, sure, let's aim for it, but buckle your seatbelt. That's honeymoon talk. And here comes the big finale: "It always protects, always trusts, always hopes, always perseveres. Love never fails" (vv. 7–8 NIV).

Right. But our marriages are filled with love that falters, with love that falls so far short of what is described in these verses that it seems almost out of place even to read them during the ceremony.

Unless they do not describe human love at all.

My inner wedding skeptic was demolished by the realization that 1 Corinthians 13 describes an *always and never* love—the kind of love that can be attributed only to a God of infinite sameness. It describes not human love, but the love for which all human hearts long: the *always and never* love of God. Only God can say with utter truthfulness that his love *always* protects, *always* trusts, *always* hopes, *always* perseveres. Only God can rightly say that his love *never* fails. What better passage to read at a wedding than one that describes the kind of love we can never hope to receive perfectly from anyone but our heavenly Father? How much more willing might we be to replace the *always and never* language of our human arguments for the language of grace and forgiveness if we could just recognize that we cannot ask another human to be our God?

Idolatry takes hold of you and me when we depend on a human relationship, a circumstance, or a possession to *never* leave nor forsake us, to *always* remain. Idolatry takes hold of us when we believe that a difficult relationship or circumstance will never change, will always be hopeless, wounding, or sorrowful. But here is truth to topple idols:

Every circumstance you encounter will change except the circumstance of your forgiveness.

Every possession you own will pass away except the pearl of your salvation.

Every relationship you enter into will waver except your adoption by your heavenly Father.

As I write, I am at the end of a week full of historic news headlines. Issues of race, gender, sexuality, religion, and politics have all erupted into chaos at the same time. Leaders have fallen, laws have been overturned, citizens have practiced civil disobedience, terrorism has inscribed its message in blood across three continents, and social media wants desperately to convince me that this time it is serious, the sky is really falling. I remember other weeks like this, the anxiety and alarm they bred in me, the gut-gripping fear. But this week I find myself in a different place, and it cannot be by accident. The raging of the nations can be navigated only by keeping a fixed point in view: the Lord God, seated on his throne. That fixed point has been my meditation this week for the sake of writing this book, and the effect it has had on my composure in the face of change and upheaval has taken me by surprise. The *always* and *never* of my unchanging God are particularly practical to me this week, and particularly precious.

There is no rock but the Rock of our salvation. No human heart is so hard that he cannot soften it, not even yours. Turn loose of the idolatry of your *always and nevers*. Those words are true only of God. Ask him to sustain you through the ever-changing moments of this life. Ask him to change what you have believed to be beyond the power of his grace to alter. Our God of infinite sameness is a rock. When all around us is shifting sand, may we cry to him: "Lead me to the rock that is higher than I, for you have been my refuge" (Ps. 61:2).

Verses for Meditation

Psalm 18:31	Matthew 7:24–27	Hebrews 13:8
Malachi 3:6	1 Corinthians 13:4–8	James 1:17

Questions for Reflection

1. How is the knowledge that God does not change reassuring to you? How might it be a caution to you as well?

2. What human relationship, possession, or circumstance do you cling to for stability instead of to our unchanging God? How reliable have you found that "substitute rock" to be?

3. How prone are you to use *always* or *never* language in an argument? What might this tendency reveal about the state of your belief?

4. What *always* or *never* have you wrongly believed to be true of yourself? Of someone else? Of a circumstance or relationship?

Pray

Write a prayer to the Lord confessing one thing about yourself you have believed to be unchangeable. Ask him for an awareness of where you have grown hardened and for grace to learn to change. Thank him for the great gift of human changeability. Praise him that he, the Lord, does not change.

7

Omnipresent

The God of Infinite Place

Within thy circling power I stand;
On every side I find thy hand;
Awake, asleep, at home, abroad,
I am surrounded still with God.

Isaac Watts

Located in the southwestern region of the United States is a tourist attraction that draws thousands of visitors every year. A six-hour drive from the nearest major airport and thirty-three miles from the nearest town, it is quite literally in the middle of nowhere. It claims no majestic rock formations or redwoods. It lures with neither canyons nor desert vistas. Resting in an unremarkable landscape, its focal point is nothing more than a small brass disc, roughly three inches in diameter—a government survey marker designating the point at which four different state

93

boundaries meet: Arizona, Utah, Colorado, and New Mexico. Tourists pose for photographs on all fours—feet in two states, hands in two more—faces beaming with the delight of being able to boast they are in four places at once.

The glee in the faces of those posing at the Four Corners Monument reveals our awareness of a very specific limit: We humans are limited to one location. The fact that we inhabit a body means we cannot be in more than one place at one time. We can move from one place to the next, but we cannot occupy two spaces simultaneously, much less four. Yet people line up to have their photo made at a spot that offers a loophole, at least in theory. We know we can be in only one place at one time, but we're fascinated by the thought that perhaps even that limit could be broken.

A body is a set of limits. Our height determines the limit of what we can see standing in a crowd. Our mass determines the limit of how much water we will displace when we step into a swimming pool. Genetics—or more properly, God—determines our arm-span and the size of our shoes. By tethering our spirits to a body, God decrees that we will be present where we are present, and nowhere else. Yet God, who is spirit, is able to be everywhere fully present. We capture this idea by attaching the prefix *omni* to the word *presence*. *Omni* literally means "all," but the easiest way to read it is to substitute *limitless* in its place—God is omnipresent, limitlessly present. No physical body limits him to a particular place.

In John 4, Jesus holds a well-known conversation with a Samaritan woman, which points out the difference between God and man in matters of place. The woman says to Jesus, "Our fathers worshiped on this mountain [Mt. Gerizim], but you say that in Jerusalem is the place where people ought to worship" (v. 20). She is asking Jesus to clarify which location is the true habitation of God. Jesus responds that "God is spirit, and those who worship him must worship in spirit and in truth"(v. 24). God, who does not have a body, is not bound by place. He is everywhere, and can therefore be worshiped anywhere. Jesus echoes the thoughts of his ancestor, King Solomon, at the dedication of the temple: "But will God indeed dwell on the earth? Behold, heaven and the highest heaven cannot contain you; how much less this house that I have built!" (1 Kings 8:27).

God, unbound by a body, is not limited to one place. He is not merely big, he is uncontainable, able to be present everywhere.

Immanent and Transcendent

Think you're cool for being able to contort your body so it touches four states simultaneously? God is present in all places all the time. Not only that, but everywhere he is present he is *fully* present. He is not engaged in some cosmic game of Twister, trying to stretch himself between an infinite number of locations. Rather than a small part of him occupying each place he inhabits, all of God is present everywhere, all the time.

But it gets crazier: All of God is fully present in all places past, present, and future. Theologians call this his *immanence*. Put simply, there is no place—or time—where God is not.

The summer after my sophomore year of college I studied abroad in France. I kept a journal as part of my classwork, and also because I wanted to remember the trip in detail. I wrote about the Eiffel Tower, the Loire Valley, the Arles Amphitheatre. Several decades later, I need that journal to recall the details of my trip. God, on the other hand, does not keep a travel journal. God does not travel. He does not need to re-member the Eiffel Tower, nor does he need anyone to describe it to him—he is there. Fully present. And he is where you are right at this moment, too. Fully present. He is fully present in worlds far beyond what the Hubble Space Telescope can see and in worlds far smaller than the strongest electron micro-scope can disclose.

Yet, he is distinct from the creation he fills. Theologians call this his *transcendence*. God is fully present in his creation, but he is not his creation. The pantheist tells us that we and all cre-ation are parts of God, small pieces of the deity. The Christian believes that "in him we live and move and have our being" (Acts 17:28), yet we are we, and he is he. If we and all creation are small pieces of the deity, we and all creation are worthy of worship, and the Bible is completely wrong to condemn us for doing so. The God of the Bible is in and around all things, but he is distinct from them.

Though God is everywhere fully present, we are not always aware that he is. At times, he unmistakably declares his pres-ence to us. At other times, he does not. Whether we sense his presence or not, "he is not far from any one of us" (Acts 17:27 NIV). Though he is fully present, we may perceive only a certain aspect of his nature in a given moment. In a worship service, we may sense overwhelmingly the presence of his love. In a time of meditating on his law, we may perceive overwhelmingly the presence of his holiness. Even in hell, God is fully present, though its inhabitants perceive only his wrath. For the believer, eternity will be a place where we experience the presence of God to the fullest of our capability. There, we will experience him as Immanuel, God *with us* as we have only experienced him to be in a limited way during this life.

Coveting Limitlessness

Humans, unlike God, are bound to one place at one time. For most of history, this one-place boundary limited man's ability to learn and acquire knowledge, to communicate ideas, to form and maintain relationships, to protect those he loved, and to give and receive love. He was born into a family and community and stayed there his entire life. His knowledge of the world was limited to the collective knowledge base of his immediate community. Should he achieve a great philosophical discovery, it might never leave his village. His business contacts and transactions required face-to-face interaction. His circle of relationships was limited to those with whom he shared physical proximity. Should family members leave his village and move to another one, his ability to protect them or even maintain the relationship would virtually vanish.

But think how much the one-place boundary has been challenged in the last two hundred years, and particularly, in the last few decades. Advances in transportation and technology enable the spread of knowledge and ideas in a way the ancients could never have imagined. Online learning removes the barriers of place associated with getting an education. When my son developed an early interest in physics, he watched lectures on his laptop by an acclaimed MIT professor, an opportunity that would have been financially and logistically impossible twenty years ago. Anyone with a blog or a social media account can broadcast his ideas to whomever will listen. Business can be transacted electronically with no geographic constraints. Forming and maintaining relationships no longer has to happen face-to-face—it happens as easily as joining Facebook or LinkedIn. And should loved ones live in a faraway location, we have Face-Time to keep us close. If they need our help or protection, we can reach them with a text or phone call in seconds, sending resources to their aid with a few keystrokes.

So many of our technological advances have targeted diminishing the limits of the one-place boundary on humankind. We eagerly await Unbound 2.0 and 3.0, wondering what new advance will free us even further from the tyranny of our physical bodies. But not everyone is waiting for an upgrade.

Unlike us, God has no one-place limits on his ability to possess knowledge. Because God is omnipresent, he is able to be omniscient (an idea we'll explore further in our next chapter). Because he is fully present in all places, he has no boundaries of communication with his creatures—he can communicate freely at will with any or all of us in a way that even a global livestream can't mimic. He can maintain an infinite number of relationships perfectly, without Facebook or Twitter. He can perfectly protect those he loves. He can give and receive love with no boundaries whatsoever. For him, no barriers of physical distance have ever existed, no geographical boundaries prevent his influence or rule.

Which begs the question: Are we idolatrous for wanting to push back the one-place limits of our physical bodies?

Divided Affections

Think how often we find ourselves wanting to be in two places at once. My four children are very close in age, so the end of the school year finds my husband and me divvying up concerts, tournaments, and award ceremonies that overlap. But we don't just divide and conquer; we text each other updates of what is happening at whichever child's event we attended. No doubt you find yourself making similar accommodations with family, work, even church. Because the Internet allows us to work remotely, our living rooms become two places at once: a workplace and a family place. We attend one church and podcast the sermons of another church. We FaceTime our kids while we're away on business trips so we can feel like we're still at home. We combine a trip to the pool with a trip to the mall, perusing Amazon on our tablet while keeping an eye on the deep end. We call it "multitasking" or "efficiency," and it certainly can be those things. But it's important for us to do a reality check every now and then regarding what we're asking our makeshift omnipresence to give us.

Because, no matter how advanced we become, we can never be everywhere fully present. We can't even be fully present in two places simultaneously. Our attention will necessarily be divided. When I text my husband the play-by-play of the event I'm attending, reading his of the event he's watching, neither of us is fully present where we are. When I allow work to invade home spaces unchecked, I stop being fully present in my living room as the parent or the spouse. When I become too absorbed with Facebook friendships, I don't invest in face-to-face friendships as I should. When I tell myself that FaceTime is just as good as being there, I'm in trouble. There is no substitute for actual face time, for one-to-one human interaction.

Think how often we hear stories of texts or emails that were misunderstood by the recipient. More often than not, someone tried to have a conversation at a distance that should have been held face-to-face. Even the New Testament authors recognized the importance of being present for significant conversations: "Though I have much to write to you, I would rather not use paper and ink. Instead I hope to come to you and talk face-to-face, so that our joy may be complete" (2 John 12). Complete relational joy occurs face-to-face, in shared physical space. When we truly care about depth of communication, we leave as little physical room for misunderstanding as possible. There is no such thing as human omnipresence. Our newfound ways to mimic it are not the same as being there. They are not a replacement for face-to-face, for being present. They aren't idolatrous in and of themselves, but they can become so when we start believing them to be equivalent to *actually being there*. They are good gifts until we ask them to make us like God.

Wanting to be in two places is not a new sensation for humans. It is a part of the human condition, particularly for parents. It is aptly reflected that having a child is like choosing to have your heart walk around outside of your body forever. Anytime we love people deeply and they are parted from us, whether temporarily or permanently, we naturally desire to be in two places at once. The apostle Paul expressed this in his letter to the Philippians: "My desire is to depart and be with Christ, for that is far better. But to remain in the flesh is more necessary on your account" (Phil. 1:23–24). Longing to cast off our one-place limit can actually be God-honoring when framed in the right motive and held in the proper perspective.

Paul expressed a desire to be "with Christ," though no doubt he knew and believed Jesus's promise to be with us always. Paul is eager for the time when his experience of the presence of Christ will be unclouded by the limits of his time-bound existence. And this is the challenge for the believer this side of eternity: we cannot trust our perception of God's closeness to be accurate. God is near whether we feel him to be or not. How mindful we are of this truth will directly affect the way we live.

Vigilance and Assurance

On the one hand, the knowledge of God's presence should make us vigilant about sin. Like a child who reaches for the cookie jar thinking his mother is out of the room, when we grow forgetful that God is everywhere fully present, we become a law unto ourselves. We tell ourselves that no one sees, that we won't get caught, that there are no consequences for the sin that goes unwitnessed. But nothing we do goes unwitnessed: "'Am I only a God nearby,' declares the LORD, 'and not a God far away? Who can hide in secret places so that I cannot see them?' declares the LORD. 'Do not I fill heaven and earth?' declares the LORD" (Jer. 23:23–24 NIV).

In recent years our world has become more and more populated with cameras. Almost everywhere we go we are being filmed. When NFL running back Ray Rice knocked his wife unconscious in a hotel elevator in 2014, he believed no one would see. But the presence of a security camera meant that his actions were broadcast to millions of viewers once the footage was leaked. The eyewitness account has been a powerful legal tool for as long as laws have existed, though human eyewitness accounts haven't always proved to be reliable. Surveillance cameras, however, don't lie. They teach a lesson about omnipresence to anyone paying attention. While governments must decide the appropriate boundaries for a citizen's privacy, no privacy laws exist between Creator and creature. More reliable than any camera is the eyewitness account of an omnipresent God.

Because of this, every sin we commit is first and foremost a sin against God. David acknowledges this in his confession in Psalm 51:4:

> Against you, you only, have I sinned
>   and done what is evil in your sight,
> so that you may be justified in your words
>   and blameless in your judgment.

John Piper notes, "Sin, by definition, is a vertical phenom-enon."[1] Jesus also points to this truth in the way he crafts the confession of the Prodigal Son. Note the order of the son's words: "Father, I have sinned against heaven and against you" (Luke 15:18 NIV). If sin were merely a matter of offending other people, if confession were merely a matter of seeking human for-giveness, grace would not be amazing. It is divine grace, freely given by a God who stands witness to the evil we have done *in his sight*, that teaches our hearts to fear and tremble in right reverence.

The fact that he is witness to our every foible and sin, public and private, should inspire us to vigilance. It should elicit from us confession and repentance. The fact that he witnesses our invisible thoughts before they turn to actions and our words before they are fully formed on our tongues should cause us to think and speak with care. The fact that he sees all, yet, against all expectation, stands ready to forgive should awaken a grati-tude of the deepest kind, a desire to be the same person in public that we are behind closed doors—a person who thinks, acts, and speaks as one who fears the Lord. A person who understands that the limitless presence of God leaves no allowance for a life of practical atheism—professing that an omnipresent God exists and then living as if he does not.

God sees. God is present. Nothing is hidden. And this is cause not just for vigilance but for assurance, the most blessed assurance the human heart can know.

When our hearts deceive us with the lie that God is distant, when we begin to wonder if our sorrows are unseen or our sins are disqualifying, we can cling to the assurance of Psalm 23: "Even though I walk through the valley of the shadow of death, I will fear no evil, for you are with me." The "with me" of God does not depend on our worthiness but his will. He wills that his chosen children will never be left alone.

There is this idea called "the ministry of presence." Those who have suffered a tragic loss of some kind can tell you about it. It occurs when people who love you come to sit by your side in the midst of your tragedy. At the moment when no well-meant words can offer you comfort, when no considerate casserole can fill your acid stomach, and no kindly sent floral arrangement can mask the pungency of your despair, they take a seat next to you and offer the silent assurance of proximity, the gift of nearness. They have come and they will not leave. Your towering, monstrous sorrow fills them neither with terror nor revulsion. Even if you pushed them away, begged them to leave, they would refuse for the good of your soul.

There is this idea called "the ministry of presence," and God is perfect at it.

"It is the LORD who goes before you. He will be with you; he will not leave you or forsake you. Do not fear or be dismayed" (Deut. 31:8). When tragedy comes, whether we battle sin or sorrow, we never face these foes alone. His spirit, which hems us in behind and before, also indwells us. He is all around us, and he is in us. How secure are we?

His certain presence is not merely a comfort in sorrow or distress, it is a comfort in the mundane and the joyful as well. He does not need to greet you in the morning with, "How did you sleep?" or in the evening with, "How was your day?" He has been with you for all of it. He never needs to catch up on your latest news or be shown your latest accomplishment. As my children are beginning to leave home for adulthood, I can feel a pull to want to be with all four of them wherever they go. It feels so odd that they are learning new ideas and experiencing life without me there to witness every moment. I know this is the natural next step, but the separation is still a loss. The nature of our fellowship has been altered. By contrast, the nature of our fellowship with our heavenly Parent undergoes no separation. It will certainly undergo alteration, but only from lesser to greater. We can know his presence during this life, and we can grow in our awareness of it, but we will know it with far greater clarity in eternity. Lord, haste the day!

Toppling the Myth of Human Omnipresence

In Genesis 28 we find Jacob fleeing from the home of his youth to escape the brother he deceived. His life thus far has been marked by self-elevation, entitlement, and cunning. Lying down to sleep, he sees a vision of heaven, with angels ascending and descending. He awakes, and exclaims, "Surely the LORD is in this place, and I did not know it" (v. 16). Indeed, his life has demonstrated a lack of acknowledgement of his ever-present God. Like Jacob, you and I must live as those who recognize that the Lord is surely present. We live as those awakened from a dream, confident that whatever place we come to, whether dark or light, near or far, frightening or safe, he is there.

No, we cannot be in more than one place at one time. When we reach for omnipresence ourselves, we guarantee that we will be fully present nowhere, spread thin, people of divided attentions, affections, efforts, and loyalties. Better to trust that these bodies which tether us to one location are good limits given by a good God. Better to marvel that, wherever we are tethered, his spirit surrounds us and fills us. Aware that he is witness to all we think, speak, and do, we learn to live circumspectly. Aware that he views his children through the lens of grace, we learn to choose frank confession over futile concealment. Aware that we cannot outrun his presence, we cease running, and abide. We learn to savor his nearness. No more virtual Twister. When we trust him as fully present everywhere, we are finally free to be fully present wherever he has placed us—face-to-face with those we love, seeking the face of God.

Verses for Meditation

1 Kings 8:27	Isaiah 66:1	Acts 17:27–28
Psalm 139:7–10	Jeremiah 23:23–24	

Questions for Reflection

1. Which of the ways we try to mimic omnipresence can you most relate to? Which of your primary relationships most needs you to be more fully present than you have been?

2. Is feeling distant from God always an indicator that something is "off" with your relationship? What factors might prevent you from feeling close to God, even if you understand on an intellectual level that you are?

3. How does the fact of God's omnipresence change the way you think about your secret sins? About the shape confession should take?

4. How does the fact of God's omnipresence comfort you personally? How does it expand your amazement at divine grace?

Pray

Write a prayer to the Lord confessing your desire to be in more than one place at one time. Ask him to help you live as one whose every moment is witnessed by an ever-present God. Thank him for the assurance that he views your thoughts, words, and deeds through the lens of grace. Praise him that there is nowhere he is not.

8

Omniscient

The God of Infinite Knowledge

He knows, yes, he knows,
Why not trust in him then,
And confide joys and woes
To the Savior of men?

Georgia C. Elliott

Every elementary school has its share of colorful characters, and mine was no different. The most annoying girl in my first grade class had pigtails, knobby knees, and a serious self-control problem when it came to answering questions. She would lean forward, flailing her arm to catch the teacher's attention before anyone else. If our teacher, Mrs. Walker, called on a different student, Miss Pigtails would stretch as far out of her seat as she could and wiggle her fingers frantically, jiggling and whispering "um-um-um-um-um" under her breath, hoping the first respondent would go down in flames. Called on at last, she would blurt out her answer with the force of a tire having a blow-out, her facial expression dissolving into triumph and relief, its effect only slightly diminished by the fact she was missing all eight of her front teeth at once.

She was a know-it-all and a smarty-pants. And she was me.

At last, Mrs. Walker pulled me aside and asked, "Doesn't it feel wonderful to give the right answer to a question?"

Yes. Yes it did. It felt truly wonderful.

"Let's allow some of the other children the chance to feel wonderful for having the right answer, too. Okay?"

Well, Mrs. Walker, frankly, it's going to be tough to sustain my giant ego under those parameters. But I see your point.

Most of us had moments growing up when we were too big for our britches. The arrogance of youth follows us into early adulthood, where the realities of life begin their corrective work of teaching us the limits of our expertise. As Mark Twain has famously noted, "When I was a boy of 14, my father was so ignorant I could hardly stand to have the old man around. But when I got to be 21, I was astonished at how much the old man had learned in seven years." Getting older means growing in knowledge, but it also means growing in our awareness of just how little we really know of all there is to know. Which is a lot. Miss Pigtails is planted squarely in middle age now, a stage at which I had expected to begin to feel a sense of assurance resulting from the life experiences and education I have accumulated. Instead, I find an increasing sense of how little I have learned and how much I still don't know. Not only that, but I have begun to forget.

The God Who Does Not Learn

Who is the smartest person you have ever known? Not the biggest smarty-pants, but the most intellectually skilled thinker? In my case, it's my grandfather. A devout man of faith, he was a nuclear engineer before the field actually existed. He accumulated patents and well-deserved accolades throughout a career that stretched well into his eighties. He died at the age of ninety-three, still the proprietor of an active mind. At his funeral, those he had mentored affectionately described him as someone so brilliant he had no doubt forgotten more science than they could hope to learn in their lifetimes. But even the smartest person I have ever known offers only the faintest shadow of the God he worshiped.

God is not merely knowledgeable; he is omniscient—limitless in his knowing. He knows all things, not because he has learned them, but because he is their origin. God does not learn. Learning implies change, and as we've already considered, he is unchanging. Learning implies the movement of a knowledge boundary, and his knowledge is unbounded. The truism, "You learn something new every day" does not apply to him at all. He has not learned one new thing ever. Unbound by time, God knows all things past, present, and future, as well as all things existing outside of time. And he never forgets, because he is everywhere fully present. We have considered with regard to his incomprehensibility that he holds perfect knowledge both of himself and of us. But this is just the beginning of the extent of what he knows. A. W. Tozer gives us this lyrical attempt at capturing the depths of the knowledge of God:

> God knows instantly and effortlessly all matter and all matters, all mind and every mind, all spirit and all spirits, all being and every being, all creaturehood and all creatures, every plurality and all pluralities, all law and every law, all relations, all causes, all thoughts, all mysteries, all enigmas, all feeling, all desires, every unuttered secret, all thrones and

dominions, all personalities, all things visible and invisible in heaven and in earth, motion, space, time, life, death, good, evil, heaven, and hell. Because God knows all things perfectly, He knows no thing better than any other thing, but all things equally well. He never discovers anything. He is never surprised, never amazed. He never wonders about anything nor (except when drawing men out for their own good) does He seek information or ask questions.[1]

Though learning is wholly foreign to God, it is wholly foundational to being human. It begins even before we are born— our mother's womb is our first classroom. It's where our five senses begin processing stimuli.[2] And we never stop learning. The statement "You're never too old to learn" was true of my grandfather, and I pray it will be true of me as well. From cradle to grave, learning is essential to being human. Not only that, it is a human right. The United Nations views education as "a fundamental human right and essential for the exercise of all other human rights."[3] When we want to deny someone the full practice of their humanity, withholding learning from them is often a measure we employ. Women, the poor, even entire ethnic populations have been kept uneducated for the purpose of control or marginalization. To be human is to learn. To deny human learning is to set ourselves up as God, albeit a malevolent version of him. Only a benevolent God can set the limits of human understanding in places that are right and good.

Testing Our Learning Limits

God has left the universe open to our exploration. We are free to discover what we may, according to our intellectual abilities, in the times and places he has ordained for us. While it may be unclear if God has placed limits on how much knowledge the human race can explore, he has clearly placed limits on how much knowledge any one human can consume and use. These limits are becoming increasingly apparent to those of us living in an age of information explosion. Thirty years after the Internet's inception, it's estimated that 39 percent of the world's population (2.7 billion people) uses it.[4] And the amount of data we generate is staggering. Every minute, email users send 204 million messages, Pinterest users pin 3,472 images, Google receives over 4 million search queries, and Facebook users share 2.5 million pieces of content.[5]

We are testing the limits of our consumption in a way previous generations have not. The Internet offers an all-you-can-eat buffet to everyone from the genuinely inquisitive to the simply bored. And we are bellying up to the buffet line as though our brains have room for (and use for) whatever we feed them. As with all buffets, though wonderful in their accessibility and variety, thoughtless consumption can lead to health problems. There is a difference between healthy learning and information gluttony: one is about being fully human, and the other is about craving limitlessness.

Our insatiable desire for information is a clear sign that we covet the divine omniscience. We want all the facts, but as finite beings we are not designed to have them. And so, not surprisingly, unmeasured consumption of information brings us not increased peace of mind, as we had hoped, but increased dissonance. Psychologists have coined a term to describe what happens when we ignore good boundaries for what we feed our brains: *information overload*. Studies show that information overload causes irritability, anger, lethargy, listlessness, and sleeplessness. It can cause elevated blood pressure, cardiovascular stress, digestive disorders, headaches, stomach pain, muscle pain, and vision problems. It affects our cognition, and thereby our productivity, shortening our attention spans and diminishing our ability to concentrate.[6]

Counterintuitively, information overload also diminishes our ability to make decisions. While fact-gathering can help us make decisions, with so many conflicting or competing facts to weigh, we bog down. We suffer "paralysis by analysis," always fearing there is another piece of information that will invalidate our current choice. Unable to weigh the seemingly endless pros and cons of any given decision, we never decide. Inaction results.[7]

But information overload also has another devastating effect: it kills empathy. Research conducted by the University of Southern California revealed that rapid exposure to headlines or stories of disasters or human tragedy can numb our sense of morality and breed indifference. According to USC sociologist Manuel Castells, "In a media culture in which violence and suffering becomes an endless show, be it in fiction or in infotainment, indifference to the vision of human suffering gradually sets in."[8]

God help us if believers disregard good boundaries for our minds. God help us if the church succumbs to inaction and indifference in the face of human suffering. We must observe God's good boundaries for how much information we can process, and how much time it takes to process it in ways that result in action and empathy.

Not a New Addiction

To be sure, we have knowledge more readily available than previous generations (it is quite literally at our fingertips), but an unhealthy desire for it is certainly not new. Humans have always believed that more knowledge is the solution to our dissonance. Take, for example, Adam and Eve, who reached for knowledge they were not designed to have. The author of Ecclesiastes, writing three thousand years before the Internet or the iPhone, concluded his reflections on the futility of human life with this observation: "Of making many books there is no end, and much study is a weariness of the flesh" (Eccles. 12:12). There is nothing new under the sun (1:9). To reach reflexively for limitless knowledge is to take our place in a timeless tableau of knowledge-grasping. Like every person before us, we think the tree of the knowledge of good and evil should be ours, nursing the belief that all knowledge should belong to us, the suspicion that God is holding out on us, the desire to know what he knows, the hunger to be like him.

Though we may be slow to recognize our craving as delusional, marketers are happy to state the obvious. A few years ago, Motorola's Droid campaign positioned its phone as "all-knowing, all-seeing." But perhaps even more to the point, albeit more subtle, is Apple's ad campaign. There is a good reason Apple's products (iPod, iTunes, iMac, iPhone) all share a common lowercase letter. At first glance, we assume that letter *i* stands for "information," but, of course, it doesn't stand for anything. Information is not what Apple's products make much of. They make much of "I." In response to Moses's magnificent rhetorical question, "Who is like you, O LORD?" (Ex. 15:11), Apple has blithely and unflinchingly answered as all humanity has since the garden: iAm.

To be clear, marketers are not the problem. Nor are the technologies they sell, or the information exchange they enable. Who is the problem? iAm. I and my desire to be limitless. If only we could discern our motives as clearly as Apple and Ecclesiastes do. But the information buffet beckons, luring us toward a perpetual feast of facts and minutiae whose scope approaches infinitude. Dazzled, we have not the presence of mind to turn to our devices and ask, "Is not this thing in my right hand a lie?" (Isa. 44:20 NIV).

We believe the lie. We believe that if we have access to limitless information we will have more peace of mind. But has our information gluttony done anything to relieve our anxieties or increase our certainty? Instantly knowing the best driving routes, who starred in what movie, where the nearest Starbucks is, or the average temperature in Zurich gives us a sense of increased control . . . for a while. But take away our connectivity and we find that our anxieties lurk right beneath the surface.

None of Our Business

The link between anxiety and not-knowing also shows itself in our craving for knowledge of the future. Like an impatient reader who flips to the last page of a suspenseful novel to relieve the tension, we want a peek into what's next. It's no wonder the practice of divination stretches back to the earliest days of human history, and it still dogs us today. For the unbeliever, it's horoscopes, palm readings, and tarot cards. For the believer, it's much the same thing, loosely draped in religious trappings: asking God for an extrabiblical sign, claiming a Bible promise out of context, or attaching significance to dreams or "prophetic words."

The Bible recounts instances in which God gave knowledge of the future to certain people for a specific purpose, but these instances cannot be taken as normative. We tell ourselves that if we knew the future, we would put that knowledge to good use, but how likely is that? It's far more likely that we would use that knowledge to stoke the flames of our self-reliance and to forward our own interests. We want to say that knowledge of tomorrow would remove our anxieties, but this assumes that tomorrow holds sunshine, or that knowing what it holds means we could face it better. Whatever tomorrow holds, we can be certain that its contents will raise as many questions as they will answer. We can trust God to manage the future without our help. It is none of our business.

But the future is not the only place we look for knowledge that isn't ours to manage. We often exhibit an unhealthy interest in the affairs of others. The Bible terms this "meddling." It is significant that Peter places meddling in the midst of a list of sins that includes murder and theft (1 Pet. 4:15). It is a form of violation of another person made in the image of God. Meddlers believe they are entitled to knowledge of other peoples' situations. While they would no doubt fiercely defend their own right to privacy, they extend no such grace to others. If information is accessible, they view it as fair game. They are the consumers of tabloid journalism, the whisperers of gossip, the curators of the secret details of other people's lives. They are the reason we have passwords on our phones and our computers.

Meddling can be tricky to catch because it often masquerades as loving concern. As a parent, I have felt the desire to meddle grow as my children have grown. The closer they move toward adulthood, the less I can (and should) be involved in their private conversations and affairs. But it has been a challenge to move from a place of knowing their every move and every word to an age-appropriate place of not-knowing. Yes, I could read every text and email on their phones. Yes, I could stalk all their online relationships and monitor all their movements by GPS. There are seasons and circumstances in which these measures may be a means of protection and blessing, but as my children mature, I must increasingly release them to God's care, trusting the all-knowing One to watch over them. We all have relationships that we feel compelled to overmonitor—a spouse, a friend prone to crisis, even someone we admire or envy. But when we meddle, we multiply their troubles and ours.

Let Go and Trust

Rather than casting all your anxieties on the Internet, which cares for no man, cast them on God, for he cares for you (1 Pet. 5:7). Rather than obsessing over the future, learn contentment in your God-ordained innocence of what is to come. Rather than meddling, focus on your own concerns. We need to let God be the one who manages all knowledge. Only he is capable, and only he can be trusted to do so with perfect wisdom. And we need to look to the knowledge of who God is to remove our anxieties. This will mean less time chasing curiosities online and more time mining for treasure in Scripture. It will mean leaving the knowledge of the future in the hands of the God who is already there. It will mean minding our own business instead of meddling. Our comfort lies not in holding all knowledge, but in trusting the One who does.

When you trust God as omniscient, you recognize and relax into four beautiful truths:

1. You cannot outsmart God. You cannot teach him a lesson of any kind. He holds all the facts. You cannot circumvent his logic or come up with an alternative or better plan. But you don't need to. Because he knows all potential outcomes and consequences, his ways are best. They are trustworthy and safe. "This God—his way is perfect; the word of the Lord proves true; he is a shield for all those who take refuge in him" (Ps. 18:30).

2. You cannot bargain with God. Because he knows exactly how you will act in every if-then scenario, you cannot convince him to act a certain way by presenting him an offer of conditional obedience or reward. Any argument you present cannot offer any new insight to him. And as we've already seen, you have nothing he needs—he doesn't need your obedience and he already owns your stuff. But you don't need to bargain with God. He has already covenanted to do and allow only what is best for you. He has sealed that covenant with the blood of Christ, shed on your behalf. "For I am sure that neither death nor life, nor angels nor rulers, nor things present nor things to come, nor powers, nor height nor depth, nor anything else in all creation, will be able to separate us from the love of God in Christ Jesus our Lord" (Rom. 8:38–39).

3. You cannot fool God. All acting, from the smallest posturing to the greatest pretense is obvious to him. To God, we are all bad actors. No one is up for an Academy Award. We are completely transparent in every attempt to represent ourselves as something we are not. Whether it suits us to act as conquering victors or cowering victims, God knows our true measure. But you don't need to fool God. He accepts you as you are, all attempts at artifice removed. The cross effectively removes our need to overplay our strengths or our weaknesses. "You have searched me, LORD, and you know me. You know when I sit and when I rise; you perceive my thoughts from afar. You discern my going out and my lying down; you are familiar with all my ways" (Ps. 139:1–3 NIV).

4. You cannot rely on God to forget. Nor should you want him to forget. If God holds all knowledge, it follows that he is incapable of forgetting. We often wrongly believe that we need a forgetful God when it comes to the record of our sins.

Learning that God does not forget can cause alarm. If he can't forget our sins, how can he fully forgive us? But you don't need God to forget. You need him to be a God who never forgets a single thing. The Bible promises that God "remembers our sins no more," which is a figurative way to say that he does not count them against us. God's inability to forget is for our good. It means we can trust his covenant. He will never forget his promises. He will never forget us. "Can a woman forget her nursing child, that she should have no compassion on the son of her womb? Even these may forget, yet I will not forget you. Behold, I have engraved you on the palms of my hands" (Isa. 49:15–16).

Toppling the Myth of Human Omniscience

Because God holds all knowledge, we don't have to. Our lives are filled with questions awaiting answers, but not so our omniscient God. He does not suffer the anxiety of not-knowing that plagues our days. He has no cause for worry, for all is certainty to him. We live in the darkness of partial and incomplete knowledge, but to him the darkness is as light. No fact conceals itself from his eyes or buries itself in the shifting shadows of time. We are free to spend our years learning in healthy ways, seeking to expand our understanding humbly, in such a way that we are transformed not into smarty-pants, but into servants.

As you survey the information buffet, ask yourself: Will the time and attention I give to this make me more like Christ? Will it make me better able to serve God and serve others? Am I feeding my intellect in a way that enables me to love the Lord my God with all of my mind, or in a way that causes information overload? Does what I'm learning cause me to worship myself, or cause me to marvel at "the wondrous works of him who is perfect in knowledge" (Job 37:16)?

And when you face uncertainty, and the answer to every nagging question is an exasperated "God knows," set aside exasperation for assurance. *God knows.*

Resting near the end of the book of Psalms, only three verses in length, is Psalm 131. In this song, David gives a picture of a heart at rest before God, free from the anxiety of human not-knowing.

> O Lord, my heart is not lifted up;
> my eyes are not raised too high;
> I do not occupy myself with things
> too great and too marvelous for me.
> But I have calmed and quieted my soul,
> like a weaned child with its mother;
> like a weaned child is my soul within me.
> O Israel, hope in the Lord
> from this time forth and forevermore.

How different my days would be if I turned from the endless information buffet line and instead repeated to myself, "I do not occupy myself with things too great and too marvelous for me . . . hope in the Lord." How different my ability to learn what mattered would be if I were to calm and quiet my soul instead of subjecting it to a cacophony of articles that are must-reads and videos that promise to change my life at the 4:39 mark. How different my ability to perceive God would be if I traded mental hoarding, soothsaying, and meddling for a well-ordered, uncluttered mind. We have been given only so much mental capacity, and no more. Those who fear the Lord honor the limits he has placed on their minds, trusting what they do not, cannot, or should not know to the One who does, perfectly. "The secret things belong to the Lord our God, but the things that are revealed belong to us and to our children forever, that we may do all the words of this law" (Deut. 29:29).

Turned loose from the myth of human omniscience, we find we are free to mind our own business. The business of every believer is to strive to understand what God has revealed. What he has revealed is sufficient for salvation, needful for godliness, and supremely worthy of meditation. It is true, noble, right, pure, lovely, admirable, excellent, and praiseworthy. It becomes the filter through which we learn to choose wisely what additional knowledge is good for our souls. And in choosing well, we employ our minds in loving God as they ought.

Think on these things.

Verses for Meditation

Job 37:16	Psalm 139:1–4
Psalm 94:9–11	Isaiah 40:27–28

Questions for Reflection

1. What kind of knowledge do you crave the most? How can you discern whether your hunger for it is healthy or unhealthy?

2. How is having information at our fingertips a blessing? How might we make better use of it to glorify God and bring about his will on earth?

3. What boundaries do you need to set with regard to information consumption? Where are you most thoughtless in your consumption patterns?

4. How does the fact of God's omniscience comfort you personally? How does it expand your amazement at divine grace?

Pray

In the space below, write a prayer to the Lord confessing your desire to know more than you need to. Ask him to help you cultivate a well-ordered mind that knows its limits and trusts the unknown to him. Thank him for the assurance that he knows all things about you and loves you unswervingly. Praise him that he knows all things perfectly.

9

Omnipotent

The God of Infinite Power

Most High, omnipotent, good Lord,
to thee be ceaseless praise outpoured,
and blessing without measure.

St. Francis of Assisi

I am positively phobic about tornadoes. When I hear the tornado sirens sound, even if I know it's high noon and blue skies and it must be a test, I get weak-kneed and crazy-eyed, and beat a path for the nearest interior room. A few stormy springs ago, the sirens sounded while I was at work. I work at our church, which is in a converted grocery store. My office space is on the second floor and bears absolutely no resemblance to a safe room. White-faced and clutching my purse, I was making a dash for the first-floor bathrooms when I bumped into a coworker ambling the opposite direction.

"Maybe we're about to meet Jesus!" she said serenely.

Honestly. Sometimes working in a church is almost too much. Politeness failed me.

"You go meet him," I squawked. "I'll be in the ladies' room lashed to the plumbing by my purse strap."

Because the plumbing is all that will be left. I know this. I remember that United Grocery Store on Jacksboro Highway like it was yesterday—a slab with a few pipes sticking up where the restrooms used to be. The morning of Tuesday, April 10, 1979, started out unremarkably in my hometown of Wichita Falls, Texas. By midafternoon, the skies had turned stormy, and our attention was fixed on the small television set scrolling a familiar list of North Texas counties across the bottom of the screen: Foard . . . Hardeman . . . Wilbarger . . . Wichita. West to east. Take cover. By the end of the day, thirteen separate tornadoes would touch down in our area, and an F4 funnel cloud a mile and a half in width would tear through my hometown, leveling a path eight miles in length.

I was four blocks from the destruction, far enough away to be spared, close enough to hear the deafening freight train that wasn't a freight train and to see the circling specks of debris that were not specks. In the days that followed, we mourned the dead and marveled at the living. We got our tetanus shots from the Red Cross and helped our friends search through chaos for their photo albums and their family pets. We pondered what mattered most and how little we understood the whys and the whos and the wheres of tragedy. We learned about power and about powerlessness.

Outer Fringes

So it's no surprise I get twitchy during tornado season. And it's no wonder I have always liked the story in the Gospels in which

Jesus awakens from a nap during a storm and tells nature to calm the heck down. Letting the curtain fall back momentarily on his divine nature, he speaks, and brings order from chaos. His disciples, stunned, wonder rightly, "What sort of man is this, that even winds and sea obey him?" (Matt. 8:27).

The sort of man who is fully God. Possessed of infinite power. Omnipotent. The very one who spoke order from chaos at the foundation of the world.

It is difficult for us to form an understanding of what infinite power entails. Tragedy-beset Job marvels at the knee-knocking F4 force of God displayed in nature, and concludes it shows only the barest traces of the divine power:

> And these are but the outer fringe of his works;
>> how faint the whisper we hear of him!
> Who then can understand the thunder of his power?
> (Job 26:14 NIV)

Who indeed?

In Revelation 19:6 the multitude at the marriage supper of the Lamb hails God as omnipotent: "Hallelujah! For the Lord our God the Almighty reigns." God is not merely possessed of great power, he is all-powerful, limitless in power, infinitely powerful. Because we know he creates and sustains all, it follows that all power would belong to him. Because we know God is not subject to change, we understand that his power can neither increase nor decrease. If it is true that "knowledge is power," how powerful is the One who holds all knowledge? Because God is not bound by location or time, his power is able to be exercised anywhere, any time.

Though we do not always perceive it, God's power is always active and absolutely unflagging. Unlike us, he does not need to take a break to regain his strength. He does not require sleep or rest of any kind because "he does not faint or grow weary" (Isa. 40:28). He has never needed nor taken a Sunday afternoon nap, never nodded off in the midst of reading a sentence of a favorite book. The six days of creation did not drain one iota of his power, yet, in his compassion, he set a pattern of rest on the seventh day for the benefit of his power-limited creatures.

Strong Father

Around our house, the kids figured out quickly that nighttime emergencies were better to bring to Dad than to Mom. I have a tendency either to fail to wake up or to fly out of bed with a giant gasp, wide-eyed and completely incoherent. So, upset tummies and bad dreams usually carried themselves to Jeff's side of the bed where reasonable help was more likely to be found. But even the excellent father of my children requires sleep. He still had to be roused. Our heavenly Father, on the other hand, never requires to be roused from slumber. His eyes never close in sleep. His thoughts never wander with fatigue. His arms never grow too weary to support and protect. Our heavenly Father is strong, and perpetually so.

The familiar playground taunt of "My dad can beat up your dad" reveals our inner awareness that to have a strong father is a thing to be envied. We have just such a Father. Not only that, but the intense desire an earthly parent has to protect a small child in its weakness is the faintest echo of our heavenly Father's desire to protect us in ours. The strong protect the weak, and blessed are those who understand into which category they fall. God entrusts each of us with a limited amount of strength, much as he entrusts us with other gifts. We can use that strength for good or for evil. Those who use it for good employ it to overcome personal sin and to protect the weak. History holds no shortage of stories of those who have used power for evil.

Perhaps the best known strong man of the Bible is Samson, whose story is told in Judges 13–16. Set apart from birth to be a deliverer of Israel, Samson was meant to use his divinely gifted strength to make war against Israel's enemies, the Philistines. Instead, he used it to win their favor, their belongings, and a fair number of their women. And he used it for his own vengeful agenda. In short, Samson used his God-given strength to *imitate* the Philistines rather than to *overthrow* them. He believed his strength to be the result of his obedience not to cut his hair. But he was wrong. It was, plain and simple, a gracious gift from God. Samson ends up blind and alone, drinking from the cup of powerlessness. In one final miraculous feat, he uses his restored strength to collapse a temple on his Philistine captors. The narrator reports with chilling finality that Samson killed more Philistines in his death than in his life. In other words, mighty Samson was more effective for God in his dying than in his living.

Like Samson, when we view a particular strength as the product of our obedience to God, we will use that strength to serve ourselves rather than to serve God and others. All strength, whether physical, emotional, or intellectual, can be used either to serve or to self-elevate. Persuasive speech can be used to motivate or to manipulate. Brawn can be used to protect or to brutalize. Genius can be used for common good or for control. Whatever power we possess, we face the choice of whether to use it for the benefit of others or abuse it for selfish gain. Power feels good. Will we see ourselves as stewards of power entrusted to us, or as owners of it? We will either disperse our power in the interest of honoring God or we will hoard and amplify it in the interest of mimicking omnipotence.

A discussion of how humans mimic omnipotence can be tough to narrow down. Since the fall, each of us is a power broker, looking for ways to use and amplify power for our own ends. For the sake of space, let's consider four of the most common sources of power we seek, and the implications of using them either to glorify self or to glorify God. To identify these four sources of power, we need look no further than the covers of the magazines in the grocery store checkout line. Based on their faithful report, our culture grants power to the strong, the beautiful, the wealthy, and the charismatic.

Sports Illustrated: Physical Strength as Power

We lavish glory on the physically strong among us. They wear Super Bowl rings, boast Olympic medals, endorse sport drinks. We pay a premium to watch them exhibit their dominance. But we often cross the line into idolatry of physical strength, an idolatry that filters down to the common masses in simpler forms. We see it in the way we glorify fitness, but we see it most tellingly in the way we marginalize those who do not possess physical strength: the elderly, the disabled, the unborn. We see it in the way domestic violence and violent crime overwhelmingly target women and children. Physical strength that worships self degrades into intimidation and brutality. By contrast, when we employ our physical strength to glorify God instead of self, we protect the weak among us with every bit of energy we can employ.

Women, in particular, hold a unique and important vantage point on physical power. Our biology, crafted by God, dictates that we are relatively physically weak compared to men. This is particularly true when we carry a child. A pregnant woman experiences a biologically imposed period of weakness, and is restored to strength once her child is delivered. Perfect health assumed, women live in the biological middle ground between the strongest among us (men) and the weakest among us (children). We feel compelled to nurture and protect the weak because we understand both the gift and the responsibility of physical strength in a way we cannot take for granted. But all of us, men and women, regardless of how much we can bench press or how far we can run, are called to love God with all of our physical strength. All believers are charged to pursue the true religion of visiting orphans and widows in their affliction, words of James that paraphrase easily to "looking after the weak and vulnerable" (see James 1:27).

Glamour Magazine: Beauty as Power

Our culture (and doubtless every culture) gives power to the beautiful. There's an episode of *Seinfeld* where Jerry dates a beautiful blond woman named Nikki, using her attractiveness to gain preferential treatment wherever he takes her. At one point he intentionally tests the boundaries of what she can get away with, breaking the speed limit and boasting of his top speed to the cop who pulls him over, confident that Nikki will be able to get him out of the ticket. She does, of course. We laugh at this scenario because we know it is true. The beautiful among us live a charmed existence where power is not earned or coerced, it is simply granted. Recognizing this, we are willing to spend thousands of dollars and hours of time to achieve or maintain physical attractiveness. The beauty industry feeds us the tantalizing lie that if we fix the outside, we will fix the inside. Products and services promise we will feel better if we look better, which is not entirely untrue. But for the believer, how we feel and how we look don't rank high on the list of factors that help us serve God and others as we should.

External beauty conveys privilege on the bearer, which is why aging is so hard for the beautiful person to face—it is the mandatory relinquishment of power. No matter how much plastic surgery you endure, you will not grace the cover of *Vanity Fair* at eighty-five. Contrary to what the beauty industry claims, true beauty begins with internal change, not external change. Will we content ourselves with cultivating the kind of beauty that cannot withstand the passage of time? Or will we cultivate the kind that points toward eternal purposes: the unfading beauty of a quiet and gentle spirit. True beauty has staying power. It doesn't terminate on its owner, but points others toward its origin.

Our first impression of a person's physical attractiveness is always tempered by getting to know them. Some people grow more beautiful on further acquaintance, but for others, not even flawless bone structure can compensate for the exposure of a flawed character. How hard we labor for external beauty versus internal beauty reveals where our treasure lies. But how we treat others also tells a story. Though culture grants privilege to the physically beautiful, the church is charged to show preferential treatment to everyone in our sphere of influence. We are called to notice and treasure not just the average, but those whose physical appearance causes others to recoil: the poor, the crippled, the lame, the blind. Inner beauty has eyes to see the least among us, and to see them as beautiful when others do not.

Forbes Magazine: Wealth as Power

The wealthy among us receive our admiration and our envy. Nothing opens up opportunities quite like money. We may not be Donald Trump or Bill Gates, but all of us have some experience of the power that money conveys, whether because we have it or because we don't. Wealth gets better seats at the hockey game, a better table at the restaurant, better nutrition, better health care, better education, and better clothes. Wealth stratifies society. Anyone who has managed to move up the economic ladder can sheepishly identify with the oft-repeated sentiment of writer Beatrice Kauffman, "I've been poor and I've been rich. Rich is better."[1] There is more truth there than we'd like to admit.

To be poor is to be powerless. We know this intuitively. But in an American-dream culture of "self-made" financial success stories, we can quickly grow to view our personal wealth as our rightful possession, along with the power it grants, to be enjoyed and employed solely by us and for us. Because we are not Bill Gates, we feel no heavy obligation to share the wealth we have—leave that to the multimillionaires, we've got bills to pay. It is precisely because wealth confers power that the Bible goes to great lengths to give us a correct understanding of how it is to be viewed and employed. It contains ample warnings against the greed, arrogance, and self-sufficiency that accompany wealth, as well as ample admonitions to use our wealth to care for the poor among us.

Regardless of how much money we have been given to steward, for the Christian, the question must always be, "Do I control the money, or does the money control me?" A believer who is unable to give liberally to those in need reveals that she has lost control of her role to steward the wealth entrusted to her. Those of us who have been given more than our daily bread must turn our eyes to those still waiting to receive theirs. We employ the power of our finances to elevate the condition of the financially powerless. We do so joyfully, knowing that we have nothing we did not receive from our Father in heaven.

People Magazine: Charisma as Power

We also grant power to those who have charismatic person-alities. Gifted with persuasive speech, humor, or the ability to cast a vision, they draw us in with their communication skills. They know how to work a crowd or write a book. They form networks of relationships that they use to forward their causes. They may be those who seek political glory or those who seek pulpits. They are CEOs and NFL coaches, screen actors, self-help gurus, talk show hosts, and news anchors. They have discovered the tantalizing truth that ideas and words have power both to destroy and to create. But they don't just land on magazine covers. In everyday life, they rise to the top of the mommy group, the PTA, the dinner party, or any other group they bless with their presence.

If you have the gift of a magnetic personality, you know how easily you can shift from motivation to manipulation. The charismatic person can love the sound of her own voice so much that she crosses the line from communicating truth to crowd-pleasing or crowd control, placing herself as the sun at the center of a solar system filled with admiring followers. Most of us do not have the charisma of a presidential candidate or a televangelist, but we all taste the power of personality to some extent. Believers who are extremely likable and proficient with words face the challenge of drawing others to themselves rather than to Christ. The rest of us have to guard against following the cult of personality. Wanting to be in the entourage of someone we perceive to be influential indicates a desire for collateral power.

But we must do more than be wary of worshiping those with a compelling voice. We must also remember to listen for and give voice to the needs of the voiceless as we are able. For whom might we speak? How might we mobilize others on their behalf? Use your gift of communication or winsomeness to shed light on their situation or cause. What human rights issue could use your voice or influence? What animal rights or environmental issue could you advocate for as a steward of creation? Our words have the power of life and death (Prov. 18:21). Those who recognize this delegated power will use them in life-giving ways for the voiceless.

Jesus and Power

Physical strength, beauty, wealth, and charisma—these are just a few of the most obvious sources of power we chase. We suspect that those who possess them are the recipients of divine favor, and that those who lack them are the objects of divine displeasure. It should be significant to us that during his earthly ministry, Jesus impressed or overpowered no one with his physical strength. Not one description of what he looked like is found in Scripture, other than that "he had no form or majesty that we should look at him, and no beauty that we should desire him" (Isa. 53:2). He did not possess personal wealth, nor did he use money to gain privilege. And though his ministry and message convinced many, he chose silence rather than persuasive speech when facing his accusers.

Jesus was rejected by the Jews in large part because he did not use power as they had expected. Or as they had hoped. Rather, knowing that all power belonged to his Father, he walked humbly among us, demonstrating divine power only as it served the greater purpose of his ministry, leaving for us an example of how that power is nowhere more clearly understood than through the filter of human weakness. Jesus demonstrated perfect trust in the strength of his Father.

And yet, those miracles. What must it have been like to see

Jesus speak peace to the storm? We pray that we might see miracles like that. We tell ourselves, "If I could witness a miracle like that, I would be able to lay to rest any doubt. If I could see the power of God calming the storm or raising Lazarus, belief would be simple." We crave the spectacle of it, the assurance of it. Like the Jews of Jesus's day, we want Messiah to use power according to our expectations.

It is not wrong to ask for a miracle. I have asked for a few myself. But we must remember that Jesus demonstrated power over the physical realm to point us to his power over the spiritual realm. Every visible miracle Jesus performed during his earthly ministry was a whisper. It was an outer fringe. As his parables murmured of a message deeper than harvests or homecomings, so his miracles murmured of a transformation deeper than the calming of tempest or the healing of disease. They pointed to the most dumbfounding miracle of all: the display of his power to transform the human heart from stone to flesh.

Toppling the Myth of Human Omnipotence

That our hearts could be made a dwelling place more suitable for the Spirit of the Lord than a tabernacle or a temple is miraculous on a scale we cannot fathom. That the seat of utter depravity could become the seat of utter purity boggles the mind. God Almighty places his Spirit in us, working in great power through us to accomplish his purposes. Paul prays for the saints to live in the strength of this power:

> I pray that out of his glorious riches he may strengthen you
> with *power* through his Spirit in your inner being, so that
> Christ may dwell in your hearts through faith. And I pray
> that you, being rooted and established in love, may have
> *power*, together with all the Lord's holy people, to grasp

how wide and long and high and deep is the love of Christ, and to know this love that surpasses knowledge—that you may be filled to the measure of all the fullness of God.

Now to him who is able to do immeasurably more than all we ask or imagine, according to his *power* that is at work within us, to him be glory in the church and in Christ Jesus throughout all generations, for ever and ever! Amen. (Eph. 3:16–21)

His power is at work within us. It is at work helping us to overcome sin and to grasp the extent of his love for us. We are literally thunderstruck by the display of God's power in the elements. But are we adequately amazed at the deeper truth it points to? Sometimes I need my eyes reopened to the greatest display of God's power I have ever witnessed: the transformation of my heart into his dwelling place. His power shines in my weakness, conquering the power of sin in my life. His power shines in my strength, turning it from selfish gain toward humble service. Samson may have missed the source of his strength and the purpose for which it was given, but we can heed his example and act as those who acknowledge the limitless power of our God.

The truth of God's limitless power would be absolutely terrifying were it not paired with the truth of his limitless goodness. He is no evil dictator. He who holds all power is benevolent to his core. This is why we can trust that he is able to work all things for our good. We daily witness the devastating effects of power misused by humans, and of power in natural disasters and disease wreaking havoc in a fallen world. But one day, Jesus will split the sky in power, uttering a final, "Peace, be still." Until that day, may we be strong in the Lord, armed and ready to use every ounce of our God-given strength for good.

Verses for Meditation

Psalm 147:5   Romans 1:20   Hebrews 1:3
Jeremiah 32:17, 27   Ephesians 1:18–20

Questions for Reflection

1. Of the four types of power discussed (physical strength, beauty, wealth, and charisma), which do you have experience with? Which do you wish you had more of?

2. What personal experience do you have of powerlessness? How did it teach you humility? How might that experience motivate you to act on behalf of others with the power the Lord has entrusted to you?

3. How are you most tempted to use power in unhealthy ways? Over whom or what circumstance do you most want to exercise power that is only God's to exercise?

4. How does the fact of God's omnipotence comfort you personally? How does it shape your understanding of the miracle of salvation?

Pray

Write a prayer to the Lord confessing how you have used power for selfish gain. Ask him to help you live as one who recognizes that all power is given by God to be used for his glory. Thank him for the gift of the Holy Spirit, the source of power in the life of the believer. Praise him for the humbling truth of his omnipotence.

10

Sovereign

The God of Infinite Rule

Maker, and sov'reign Lord
Of heav'n, and earth, and seas!
Thy providence confirms thy Word,
And answers thy decrees.

Isaac Watts

I have waited to talk about sovereignty until the end. As much as I might have liked to start with it, the end is where it belongs. The best storytellers of my childhood knew this to be sound practice, saving the full revelation of who is the rightful ruler until the final scenes. I'm thinking of Narnia, of course. And of Middle Earth. And *Sleeping Beauty*. And *The Sword in the Stone*. And even Star Wars, if you count Princess Leia. Such stories acknowledge the heroes' claims to the throne from the beginning, but wait to fully comprehend their majesty and authority until the closing pages, when we see them crowned and ruling at last.

Having taken our time discovering the multilayered perfections of God, we are at last ready to see him crowned and ruling, as we might not have been at the beginning. We are ready to meditate on his sovereignty. The idea of God's infinite rule is not only difficult to grasp, it is difficult to trust, unless we have first spent time considering other aspects of his nature. It would be out of order to present to you a God of infinite authority without first pointing to his omnipotence. While God's omnipotence asserts that there are no limits on his *ability* to act, God's sovereignty asserts that there are no limits on his *authority* to act. So also his omniscience, omnipresence, eternality, and immutability single him out as not just capable of ruling, but as imminently qualified to rule. Every attribute we have considered thus far has been moving us toward this inevitable conclusion: the most right and logical place for God to inhabit is a throne.

No wonder the Bible portrays him there so often. His throne is described as a place of worship and celebration, but also as a place of trembling and awe. A place of right reverence. The fear of the Lord is the beginning of wisdom. The wise see and celebrate God not just as their Father to whom they owe adoration, but as their King to whom they owe their total allegiance.

They pray, as Jesus taught them to pray, "Your kingdom come, your will be done."

Out of the Mouths of Babes

When my son Matt was small, we taught him the Lord's Prayer, that beautiful model prayer of submission to divine authority. But the King James language proved a tongue twister for Matt's

three-year-old verbal skills. So each night he would bow his head
and earnestly pray,

Odder Fodder who art in heaben,
Hallowed be my name.
My kingdom come, my will be done
on earf as it is in heaben.

It was either the most comically mispronounced prayer of all
time, or the most transparently honest one. Matt uttered aloud
the desire most of us only repeat silently in our hearts: my kingdom come, my will be done.

We want our rule. We want our kingdom, our power, our
glory. We want the very throne of God.

But we are wholly unqualified for it. Only God is. And we
have no right to it. Only God does. But where does his right
come from? Earthly sovereigns rule by right of birth, but what
about God? What gives him the right to expect and demand our
allegiance?

We owe God our allegiance for one simple reason—not because we sinned against him and feel guilty, not because he saved
us and we feel grateful—we owe him our obedience because he
made us. He holds *authority* over us because he is our *author*.
It is his natural right as our Creator. The potter forms the clay,
and the clay does not question its design or purpose.

But it has no need to—he is a good potter, and he knows
what he is doing.

Americans in particular chafe at the idea of unquestioning submission to a ruler. So steeped in democracy are we that
we feel we should get to register our vote on all of life's decisions, both individual and collective. The most cursory glance
at human history affirms that unquestioning submission to an

earthly authority is not a universally safe posture. It is a posture that invites abuse. In the hands of sinful men, authority can be (is almost certain to be?) misused. Humans with absolute authority command submission to what brings them glory, regardless of the harm it inflicts on those they govern.

But in the case of an infinitely benevolent Sovereign, our unquestioning submission is not only desirable, it is the only rational course to follow. God never requires submission to a harmful command. None of his commands are harmful. In commanding what brings him glory he commands what ultimately brings us good. He can only use his authority for good.

Casting Lots, Craving Control

Any discussion of the sovereignty of God makes me think about Bunco. Far less tawdry than its Vegas cousin, craps, Bunco is a game of chance unencumbered by excessive rules, employing a prize system instead of a betting one. You need only one skill to play: the ability to roll a pair of dice. If you roll certain number combinations, you get a hash mark. If you get the most hash marks, you advance to the coveted Winner's Table, where prizes are eventually distributed to those upon whom Lady Luck has smiled.

The first time I attended neighborhood Bunco, I learned a lesson in human nature. Despite the fact that we were clearly playing a game of chance, the woman who organized the group sat at the Winner's Table for the entire evening, consistently winning match after match. Not even a second glass of merlot blunted her competitive edge. The Bible nerd in me kept thinking, "If 'the lot is cast into the lap, but its every decision is from the LORD' (Prov. 16:33), this woman is seriously in favor with God." At the end of the evening I marveled at her brilliant defiance of the laws of probability to the friend who had invited me. My friend smirked.

"She wins every time."

"How is that even possible?" I asked.

"She cheats. She volunteers to keep score, but she makes extra hash marks in her own column. We're all scared of her, so we just let her win."

The odds of winning at Bunco (cheaters disallowed) are fifty-fifty. But the odds that any given group of people will contain a bully seeking control are, I suspect, somewhat higher. It starts on the playground and continues all the way to the boardroom and the highest levels of government. Someone is always vying for control. Someone is always looking to ascend the throne, to seek the highest place. In the previous chapter we discussed the effects of power on humans. Now we consider the effects of its close relative, authority. Whereas power is the means to effect change, authority is the right to do so, on whatever terms the one with authority chooses.

Human authority—that of governments and leaders—is delegated, granted to us temporarily by the God who holds all authority. In the Old Testament, God grants authority to both Israel and Israel's enemies as suits his purposes. In the New Testament, Jesus points out to Pontius Pilate during his trial: "You would have no authority over me at all unless it had been given you from above" (John 19:11). Romans 13:1 tells us to submit to earthly authorities: "For there is no authority except from God, and those that exist have been instituted by God." Whether earthly rulers exercise their authority for good or for evil, ultimately God is in control. Control lies at the heart of what we must understand when we speak of the sovereignty of God.

The question we must resolve regarding sovereignty is this: How much does God control?

The Bible makes the bold and repeated claim that God controls not just many things or most things, but all things. As R. C. Sproul notes, "If there is one single molecule in this universe running around loose, totally free of God's sovereignty, then we have no guarantee that a single promise of God will ever be fulfilled."[1] There are no limits on what he controls. Thus, whatever he wills, he does. He is completely free to act according to what he decrees. He requires permission from no one. Because he needs nothing from anyone, knows all things, is everywhere present, and holds all power, no one exists who could possibly trump or challenge his plans. His limitlessness in every area points to his sovereignty over all things. "Nothing can hinder him or compel him or stop him. He is able to do as he pleases always, everywhere, forever."[2]

Or, as Job put it, "I know that you can do all things, and that no purpose of yours can be thwarted" (Job 42:2).

Acknowledge Paradox, Act Practically

Because God controls all things, he can ultimately work all things for our good, even those things that others mean for evil. Theologians speak of his active will and his passive will. He works actively through our obedience, but he can also work passively through disobedience, as in the case of Joseph's brothers. Joseph recognized that God had used what they intended for evil to bring about his good purposes.

Though God controls all things, those who do evil are still accountable for their sinful choices. How can this be? How can we be responsible for our choices if God is sovereign? Divine sovereignty and human responsibility are parallel truths we must hold simultaneously. The Bible consistently affirms

God's total sovereignty and man's free will. The same Jesus who said, "No one can come to me unless the Father who sent me draws them," says, "Come to me, all you who are weary and burdened, and I will give you rest" (John 6:44; Matt. 11:28 NIV). In our fallen sinful state, we are unwilling to come to him. So God regenerates us, changing the disposition of our hearts. Then, from our own will, which is finally freed from its bondage, we willingly respond to his call to come to him and be saved. If we humans cannot make genuine and responsible choices, then God is unjust to punish sin. Indeed, he is responsible for it.

How our free will and God's sovereignty can coexist is a mystery. Any time the human and the divine intersect, paradox will appear and our human limits will obscure how two seemingly contradicting points can both be true. It is good for us to wrestle with paradox, but if we allow it to draw our eyes away from a question of more pressing concern, we miss the point. That question is this: How committed are you to the myth of your own sovereignty?

To arrive at an honest answer, consider four areas in which we strive for control.

1. Controlling Our Bodies

How we relate to our bodies reveals much about our need for control. Caring for our bodies is a stewardship issue. They are not our own. They have been given to us to maintain in healthy ways. But when we cross the line into unhealthy control, we move from stewardship to idolatry. This can take the form of obsessive concern with diet or exercise, eating disorders, excessive fear about illness or germs, hypochondria, fear of aging, or just garden variety vanity.

How can we know when we've crossed a line from steward-ing to controlling? Certainly by the impact on our time, but also by the impact on our words and our wallets. When we desire un-healthy control over our bodies, we talk about them constantly. Our methods, expectations, and results find their way into our conversations and our social media posts. We rationalize the financial cost for whatever supplement, medical procedure, anti-aging cream, smoothie maker, or gym membership is necessary to achieve our body goal.

Ultimately, our need for control impacts our relationships neg-atively. We pass judgment on those who don't follow our strict reg-imens, looking down on them as undisciplined about their health or careless about their appearance. And we prioritize our discre-tionary time and resources for ourselves instead of for others.

2. Controlling Our Possessions

Like our bodies, our possessions are ours to steward, not to do with as we please. It's not wrong to have stuff, it's just wrong to worship stuff. When we cross the line into unhealthy control, we develop obsessive concern about acquiring, multiplying, or maintaining what we have. This may manifest as hoarding, com-pulsive purchasing, fear of using what we own because it might get damaged or suffer wear, compulsively maintaining property, micromanaging finances, or the inability to loan or give items to others.

Does a scratch on your car send you into orbit? Is the fact that your car is meticulously maintained a source of pride for you? How we react to damage or loss of possessions reveals whether we have control issues in this area. Does amassing debt to maintain a certain lifestyle sound rational to you? Something may be amiss with how you view your stuff.

3. Controlling Our Relationships

Every human relationship we have is ordained by God, an opportunity to show preferential love to another person made in his image. Relationship conflict is always about control. A desire for unhealthy control in a relationship can manifest as intimidation or manipulation (verbal, emotional, physical), the hallmarks of abuse. We know what the extremes look like—we see them on the evening news, or we have the sorrow to know them firsthand. Most of us don't fit the category of "abuser," but that doesn't mean we aren't controllers on some level.

Lesser forms of control reveal themselves as an inability to admit we are wrong, a need to have the final word, a need to have the upper hand, a "my way or the highway" attitude. Whether we behave this way toward a child, a spouse, a friend, or a coworker, we are exercising control in an unhealthy way.

Nowhere is it harder not to exercise controlling behaviors than with those we have legitimate authority over. Parents, church leaders, and business leaders who love control too much will slip into an authoritarian style of leadership, one that makes rules more important than relationship. Being in authority means setting boundaries that preserve relationship. It does not mean setting boundaries that preclude relationship.

A friend once told me that when her children would tattle in the midst of a fight (a transparent battle for control), she would ask, "Who is being the kindest?" What an insightful question to ask of any relationship conflict. Preferential love of others requires crushing our desire to control them. Do you allow moodiness to make others walk on eggshells around you? Do you expect others to be able to read your mind when your feelings are hurt? Is there subtext to your speech? Choose kindness over control, and watch your relationships gain health.

4. Controlling Our Circumstances or Environments

Life is uncertain. Though God knows the future, we do not, and most of us don't deal well with ambiguity. Those who want to control circumstances attempt to account for every contingency. They habitually overplan, turning the simplest tasks into major undertakings. The less control they perceive themselves to have, the more controlling behavior they demonstrate. They backseat drive, offer unsolicited advice or "help" with projects or situations that don't involve them directly, practice slavish punctuality even when no one else is waiting for them, and fight an overpowering desire to be the person in charge of the TV remote. They know the best way to load the dishwasher, surreptitiously rearranging it when they think no one is watching.

They dig recycling out of the trash can when the party ends, no matter how late the hour or how copious the trash. They won't be able to sleep until it's done, anyway. They develop rituals and routines upon which they depend for their peace of mind. Rules exist for everything from what order to eat the food on the plate to how to properly organize a sock drawer. If a mirror is crooked on your wall, can you walk past without adjusting it? If not, maybe take some time to look into it as you do. I know I had to in order to come up with these examples. Not all of them fit me, but many of them do. No one would accuse me of being compulsively punctual, but I'm widely known to be a recycling Pharisee and a dishwasher legalist. You don't have to be diagnosed OCD to have control issues with your circumstances or environments. You just have to be a limited human.

Toppling the Myth of Human Sovereignty

When we reach for control, we announce our belief that we, rather than an all-knowing, all-seeing, all-powerful, infinitely good God, should govern the universe. Our control issues grow out of speculating about the "what if." Our inability to answer the "what if" definitively causes anxiety—anxiety about the likelihood that our kingdom shall come and our will shall be done. My husband always soothes my anxiety by pointing me back to an important question: What's your worst-case scenario? Speaking aloud my fears about circumstances, relationships, possessions, or my body helps lay them to rest. Or more precisely, it helps me lay them at the feet of my Father in heaven. It is a form of confession, letting my mouth speak out of the overflow of my heart, giving voice to my nagging fears and relinquishing my need for control. It is an acknowledgment that his is the kingdom.

> Yours, O LORD, is the greatness and the power and the glory and the victory and the majesty, for all that is in the heavens and in the earth is yours. Yours is the kingdom, O LORD, and you are exalted as head above all. Both riches and honor come from you, and you rule over all. In your hand are power and might, and in your hand it is to make great and to give strength to all. (1 Chron. 29:11–12)

So said King David to the King of heaven. So say I.

Over what do I have control? A few very important things. My thoughts, which I can take captive by the power of the Holy Spirit. And if I can control my thoughts, it follows that I can control my attitude—toward my body, my stuff, my relationships, and my circumstances. If my thoughts and attitude are in control, my words will be as well, and my actions. The redeemed obediently submit thought, word, and deed to their heavenly Ruler, trusting uncertainty to him who "works all things according to the counsel of his will" (Eph 1:11). They step away from the throne, acknowledging that they are utterly unqualified to fill it.

How long will you strive with your Maker? How long will you seek the highest place? Jesus Christ went to the lowest place so that you and I might have fellowship with God. Therefore, God has exalted him. Therefore, humble yourself. What is more beautifully humbling than relinquishing control?

The best storytellers of my childhood were on to a winning formula. Every truly good story echoes the best story of all. The Bible recounts the story of a king whose claim to a throne is recognized from the beginning, but whose majesty and authority are only fully apprehended in its closing pages, when we see him crowned and ruling at last. His faithful utterance from the throne is this: "Behold, I am making all things new" (Rev. 21:5).

"Our God is in the heavens; he does all that he pleases" (Ps. 115:3). And all that he pleases is for our good.

Verses for Meditation

Job 23:13	Psalm 115:3	Daniel 4:35
Psalm 33:11	Isaiah 14:24	Romans 9:14–21

Questions for Reflection

1. Of the four types of control discussed (body, possessions, relationships, circumstances), which do you want the most? Which is not a problem for you?

2. Over whom has God placed you in authority? To whom has God commanded you to submit? How should submitting to authority make us better at exercising it, and vice versa?

3. In what area do you feel the most out of control? What is your worst-case scenario? Confess it to God and ask him to grant you freedom from anxiety.

4. How does the fact of God's sovereignty comfort you personally? How does it shape your understanding of the miracle of salvation?

Pray

Write a prayer to the Lord confessing how you have reached for control in unhealthy ways. Ask him to help you trust and submit to his authority in thought, word, and deed. Thank him that he is making all things new. Praise him for the humbling truth of his sovereignty.

Conclusion

Fearful and Wonderful

I praise you, for I am fearfully and wonderfully made.

Psalm 139:14

If you had told me five years ago that I would one day write a book for Christian women that concluded with this particular quote from Psalm 139, I probably would have punched you in the face. Arguably no single sentence in Scripture is more heavily applied to women by other well-meaning women, but stick with me as we attempt to see it with new eyes. For the purpose of wrapping up the business at hand, I think this statement deserves a second look—for what it says about women, and more, for what it says about God.

I recently attended a women's conference with a line-up of three different speakers. In each session, each individual speaker spent time on Psalm 139:14, urging us to see ourselves the way God sees us, as fearfully and wonderfully made. It could have been just about any women's event, with just about any speaker. On a daily basis, women in our culture combat the overwhelming sense that we are not enough. Christian women often do so with Psalm 139:14. We ask it to soothe us when our body image falters, or when we just don't feel that smart, valuable, or capable. We ask it to bolster us when our limits weigh us down. But based on how frequently I hear it offered, I suspect the message may not be sticking very well.

Why is that?

I believe it is because we have misdiagnosed our primary problem. Our primary problem as Christian women is not that we lack self-worth, not that we lack a sense of significance. It's that we lack awe.

Look Up

On a recent visit to San Francisco, my husband and I had the chance to hike Muir Woods. Walking its paths, we halted, slack-jawed, to gaze up at two-hundred-and-fifty-foot redwoods that had stood since the signing of the Magna Carta. Towering and ancient, they reminded us of our smallness, that we are of yesterday. Muir Woods was a place to be awestruck. But not necessarily for everyone. I can still see the eight-year-old playing a video game while his parents took in the view. I'm not judging Mom and Dad—I've been on vacation with young children myself—but the irony of the image was compelling.

Research shows that when humans experience awe—wonderment at redwoods or rainbows, Rembrandt or Rachmaninoff—we become less individualistic, less self-focused, less materialistic, and more connected to those around us.[1] In marveling at something greater than ourselves, we become more able to reach out to others. At first, this seems counterintuitive, but on closer examination, it begins to sound a lot like the Great Command: Love God with heart, soul, mind, and strength (marvel at Someone greater than yourself) . . . love your neighbor (reach out to others). Awe helps us worry less about self-worth by turning our eyes first toward God, then toward others. It also helps establish our self-worth in the best possible way: we understand both our insignificance within creation and our significance to our Creator. But just like a child on an iPad at the foot of an eight-hundred-year-old redwood, we can miss majesty when it is right in front of us.

We do it habitually with Psalm 139:14. It's easy to hear it as a "pink verse" when a woman is reading it aloud to a room full of women. It is harder to hear it that way when we consider who wrote it. Imagine King David writing it to give himself a pep talk about his appearance or his self-worth. No, Psalm 139:14 is not written to help us feel significant. We have only to zoom out and consider the entire psalm to see this. Without question, the subject of Psalm 139 is not us. It is God.

> O Lord, you have searched me and known me!
> You know when I sit down and when I rise up;
>   you discern my thoughts from afar.
> You search out my path and my lying down
>   and are acquainted with all my ways.
> Even before a word is on my tongue,
>   behold, O Lord, you know it altogether.
> You hem me in, behind and before,
>   and lay your hand upon me.
> Such knowledge is too wonderful for me;
>   it is high; I cannot attain it.

He searches, knows, discerns—omniscient.
He is behind and before—eternal.
He is beyond human reckoning—incomprehensible.

Where shall I go from your Spirit?
>Or where shall I flee from your presence?
If I ascend to heaven, you are there!
>If I make my bed in Sheol, you are there!
If I take the wings of the morning
>and dwell in the uttermost parts of the sea,
even there your hand shall lead me,
>and your right hand shall hold me.
If I say, "Surely the darkness shall cover me,
>and the light about me be night,"
even the darkness is not dark to you;
>the night is bright as the day,
>for darkness is as light with you.

He is near and far, high and low—omnipresent.
His right hand sustains—self-sufficient.

For you formed my inward parts;
>you knitted me together in my mother's womb.
I praise you, for I am fearfully and wonderfully made.
Wonderful are your works;
>my soul knows it very well.
My frame was not hidden from you,
when I was being made in secret,
>intricately woven in the depths of the earth.
Your eyes saw my unformed substance;
in your book were written, every one of them,
>the days that were formed for me,
>when as yet there was none of them.

He creates life—self-existent.
He does wondrous works—omnipotent.
He ordains each day—sovereign.

How precious to me are your thoughts, O God!
>   How vast is the sum of them!
If I would count them, they are more than the sand.
>   I awake, and I am still with you.

He is immeasurable—infinite.

He endures—immutable.

Omniscient, eternal, incomprehensible, omnipresent, self-sufficient, self-existent, omnipotent, sovereign, infinite, immutable. No, Psalm 139 is not a psalm about me, fearfully and wonderfully made. It is a psalm about my Maker, fearful and wonderful.

It is a psalm intended to inspire awe.

Responding to Awe

But David doesn't stop with slack-jawed wonder. His awe generates a response. We reach the part of Psalm 139 that the women's conference rarely addresses. Unsuited for a coffee mug or a T-shirt, these verses jar us:

Oh that you would slay the wicked, O God!
>   O men of blood, depart from me!
They speak against you with malicious intent;
>   your enemies take your name in vain.
Do I not hate those who hate you, O LORD?
>   And do I not loathe those who rise up against you?
I hate them with complete hatred;
>   I count them my enemies.

At first, our modern ears don't know how to hear David's blood-lust for his enemies. Isn't awe of God supposed to inspire us to love others? In David's day the battle was still against flesh and blood, but in our own day, we are called to love our physical enemies and make holy war on our spiritual one—the world, the flesh, and the Devil. Our response to the awesome revelation of God's character should be to hate sin with complete hatred, with every fiber of our being, and to petition God to commit it to total destruction. But note whose sin concerns David the most in light of God's glory:

Search me, O God, and know my heart!
   Try me and know my thoughts!
And see if there be any grievous way in me,
   and lead me in the way everlasting!

Search me. Try me. Expose me. Lead me. Awe begets humility, confession, and submission.

Walk the Path

We have spent ten chapters attempting to make a start at embracing our limits in light of our limitless God. If, in considering ten things that are true only of God you have felt the awakening of awe, let your response be David's. What better worship can we offer than our willingness to see and confess sin? Our willingness to walk in the way everlasting, the path of wisdom?

Just as Psalm 139 extols the attributes of God, so does the whole of Scripture. Read it with new eyes, eyes that hunger for a loftier vision of who he is. It is the awe-laden path of wisdom, surrounded on all sides by the towering redwoods of God's majesty, leaving us weak-kneed with wonderment, filled with the fear of the Lord. Behold there your Maker, fearful and wonderful. Lift up your eyes. Don't miss the view.

The fear of the Lord is the beginning of wisdom. You stand at the trailhead—you have only to begin. May God grant you awe at every vista. May God grant you wisdom with every step.

Notes

Chapter 1: *Infinite: The God of No Limits*
1. Frederick M. Lehman, "The Love of God," 1917.

Chapter 3: *Self-Existent: The God of Infinite Creativity*
1. A. W. Tozer, *The Knowledge of the Holy: The Attributes of God, Their Meaning in the Christian Life* (New York: Harper & Row, 1961), 44.

Chapter 5: *Eternal: The God of Infinite Days*
1. "O for a Thousand Tongues to Sing," 1739.

Chapter 7: *Ominipresent: The God of Infinite Place*
1. John Piper, "How Could David Say to God—After Sleeping with Uriah's Wife and Then Killing Him—'Against You and You Only Have I Sinned'?" desiringGod.org, November 14, 2008, http://www.desiring god.org/interviews/how-could-david-say-to-god-after-sleeping-with -uriahs-wife-and-then-killing-him-against-you-and-you-only-have-i -sinned.

Chapter 8: *Omniscient: The God of Infinite Knowledge*
1. A. W. Tozer, *The Knowledge of the Holy: The Attributes of God, Their Meaning in the Christian Life* (New York: Harper & Row, 1961), 87.
2. Laura Flynn McCarthy, "What Babies Learn in the Womb: They're Doing and Thinking a Lot More Than We Used to Believe," *Parenting. com*, accessed July 21, 2015, http://www.newsmaster.be/flow/dw/ciel /2011/aout11/infooverloadbrief.pdf/.
3. "The Right to Education," UNESCO.org, accessed August 24, 2015, http://www.unesco.org/new/en/right2education.

4. Susan Gunelius, "The Data Explosion in 2014 Minute by Minute—Infographic," ACI.info, July 12, 2014, http://aci.info/2014/07/12/the -data-explosion-in-2014-minute-by-minute-infographic/.
5. Ibid.
6. Joseph Ruff, "Information Overload: Causes, Symptoms and Solutions," Learning Innovations Laboratories, Harvard Graduate School of Education, December 2002, http://www.newsmaster.be/flow/dw/ciel /2011/aout11/infooverloadbrief.pdf.
7. Margarita Tartakovsky, "Overcoming Information Overload," *Psych-Central.com*, January 21, 2013, http://psychcentral.com/blog/archives /2013/01/21/overcoming-information-overload/.
8. "Scientists Warn of Twitter Dangers," *CNN.com*, April 14, 2009, http://www.cnn.com/2009/TECH/ptech/04/14/twitter.study/index .html?_s=PM:TECH.

Chapter 9: Omnipotent: The God of Infinite Power
1. Quoted in *The Washington Post*, May 12, 1937.

Chapter 10: Sovereign: The God of Infinite Rule
1. R. C. Sproul, *Chosen By God: Knowing God's Perfect Plan for His Glory and His Children* (Carol Stream, IL: Tyndale, 1986), 26–27.
2. A. W. Tozer, *The Knowledge of the Holy: The Attributes of God, Their Meaning in the Christian Life* (New York: Harper & Row, 1961), 170–71.

Conclusion: Fearful and Wonderful
1. Paul Piff and Dacher Keltner, "Why Do We Experience Awe?" *The New York Times*, May 22, 2015, http://www.nytimes.com/2015/05 /24/opinion/sunday/why-do-we-experience-awe.html?smid=tw-share &_r=1.

Scripture Index

Personal Reflections

Personal Reflections

Personal Reflections

Personal Reflections

Personal Reflections

Personal Reflections

Personal Reflections

Personal Reflections

Personal Reflections

Personal Reflections

Personal Reflections

Go Deeper in Your Study of God's Word

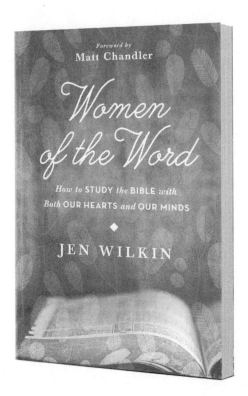

Clear and concise, this book will help you study Scripture in a way that trains your mind and transforms your heart.

crossway.org/womenoftheword

Personal Reflections